Praise

'*B2B Sales and Marketing Mastery* pr[...]
leaders with a clear and structured path to navigate
the modern B2B landscape and address its challenges
more effectively. With his energy and holistic
approach, Mads Winther brings a fresh perspective
to developing sales organizations.'

> — **Matt Dixon**, Co-founder, DCM Insights,
> and co-author of *The Challenger Sale* and
> *The JOLT Effect*

'*B2B Sales and Marketing Mastery* is a game-changer
for sales professionals and leaders looking to elevate
their approach and achieve consistent, measurable
results. Whether you're a seasoned sales leader or
just starting out in the field, you'll find the strategies
outlined in this book easy to understand and
implement. It's not just a theoretical guide—it's a
practical playbook for mastering the complexities
of B2B sales and marketing in today's ever-evolving
business environment. If you're looking for a way to
bridge the gap between ambition and results, look
no further.'

> — **Karina Burgdorff Jensen**, Assistant
> Professor, UCN Aalborg Denmark

B2B SALES AND MARKETING MASTERY

Craft your strategy, ignite your team
and turn leads into loyal customers

Mads Winther

R^ethink

First published in Great Britain in 2025
by Rethink Press (www.rethinkpress.com)

© Copyright Mads Winther

Contents

Introduction

Is your sales team struggling to close deals despite following the "best practices" you've read about and implemented? Do your marketing efforts often feel like a shot in the dark, hoping to hit a constantly moving target? Are you tired of the disconnect between your sales and marketing teams, each pointing fingers when the numbers don't add up?

You're not alone if you've answered yes to these questions.

Many business to business (B2B) sales and marketing professionals feel like they're fighting an uphill battle, navigating an ever-changing digital landscape with outdated maps. The traditional tactics that once guaranteed success are no longer sufficient. In today's competitive market, relying on what used to work is a recipe for stagnation and failure.

B2B sales and marketing have evolved, but most companies' strategies have not. The shift toward digital has changed how buyers make decisions.

Prospects are more informed, more selective, and have higher expectations than ever before. They're bombarded with content, pitches, and promises. They don't just want to buy; they want to feel understood, valued, and assured that they're making the right decision.

Yet, many sales teams still operate in silos, disconnected from the very marketing teams designed to support them. This misalignment leads to confusion, wasted resources, and missed opportunities. The lack of a unified, coherent approach leaves both sales and marketing professionals frustrated, under pressure, and unsure how to adapt to this new reality.

A proven blueprint for success

This book offers a way out of the confusion.

Drawing on my twenty-five years of experience in the B2B industry, having trained teams and lectured extensively on sales and marketing, I've developed a practical, structured framework that can transform how your organization approaches these skills. This isn't just theory; it's a tested playbook designed to drive consistent, reliable results in a digitally focused world.

When I first started thinking about this book, it was because I noticed a pattern in my work. Clients were always asking me for supplementary material to support my training lessons. They wanted a concrete guide to follow, adapt, and implement. I began my search for a suitable text that could serve that purpose and came up empty. I couldn't find one that fit my taste and philosophy. I also realized that while there was plenty of literature on business to consumer (B2C) marketing, there was a glaring gap in the B2B sector.

This book is my answer to that gap. This comprehensive guide combines strategy, structure, process, and culture in one cohesive narrative.

With over two decades of hands-on experience, I've seen what works and what doesn't. I've led teams through market shifts, technological changes, and economic challenges. I've consulted for companies large and small, helping them navigate the complexities of B2B sales. My background isn't just theoretical; it's practical and grounded in real-world experience. I've been in the trenches and know your challenges because I've faced them, too.

All this is to say that I'm not full of crap. I know my stuff.

What you'll learn

In this book, you'll discover how to:

- **Develop a winning framework.** Understand the critical elements of a successful B2B sales strategy and how to tailor them to your specific industry and market.

- **Align sales and marketing.** Create a seamless, integrated approach where sales and marketing work hand-in-hand to drive growth and achieve common goals.

- **Leverage digital tools.** Properly integrate digital marketing techniques and tools into your approach and enhance effectiveness.

- **Build a customer-centric culture.** Foster a company culture that puts the customer at the heart of everything you do, ensuring long-term success and customer loyalty.

- **Measure success.** Identify the key metrics that matter and track them to continually refine and improve your approach.

… and much more.

Throughout this book, you'll find links and QR codes to access videos that dive deeper into the topics and provide motivational insights to support your journey. These videos are optional and can be watched at any time—whether as a follow-up to a chapter or for inspiration to actively engage with the concepts. Explore them in any order that suits you.

By the end of this book, you won't just understand how to improve your B2B sales and marketing efforts—you'll have a clear, actionable plan to implement. The ideas and strategies here are designed to give you the confidence, knowledge, and tools you need to succeed.

Are you ready to take your B2B sales and marketing to the next level? Are you prepared to transform frustration into success and uncertainty into confidence?

If so, then let's begin this journey together.

You can watch the first video at https://salesmarketingmastery.com/video/welcome or scan the QR code.

PART ONE

HOW TO CRAFT A POWERFUL SALES AND MARKETING STRATEGY

W hat does a sales and marketing strategy really mean to you? Is it some magical roadmap that promises to lead you from zero to hero? Maybe it's a buzzword thrown around in boardrooms to make people feel smart.

Sure, strategy sounds like something you should have—a compass guiding you through the chaos of modern business—but here's the real question:

How do you actually create one?

It's easy to say, "We need a strategy," but how do you move beyond the buzzwords and into actionable real-world decisions? What pieces make up the puzzle? How do you know where to start, what to prioritize, and—more importantly—how do you ensure it works?

A marketing strategy isn't just a cool idea you scribble on a napkin during a late-night brainstorming session. It's an intricate dance of understanding your audience, market, competition, and even yourself. What if that dance goes wrong? You're left spinning in circles, wasting time, money, and effort—while your competitors glide past you.

This part of the book is all about crafting a winning strategy that doesn't just sound good, but actually works. We're going to break down each element. What do you need to think about? What pitfalls do you need to avoid? How do you weave all the pieces together to create a strategy that doesn't just sit on a PowerPoint slide, but drives actual results?

This is where it all begins. Ready to get started?

1
The Game Has Changed

A dmit it: things aren't the way they used to be. In fact, it seems like the game is altogether different.

A few years ago, it probably seemed like you had mastered the game of selling in your company from A to Z. Sure, you worked hard in the beginning, but once you had figured out a model for driving sales reliably, there was nothing more to do. You could sit back and wait for sales to roll in. You could provide your team with a script; if they followed it well enough, it would almost guarantee results.

What else *is* there to do? Just keep the engine running, that's all.

That's how it has always been—a smooth ride for years. You might even have started believing you had the best job in the world, but now it feels like you are playing to a different tune. You are doing the same things you've done for years, but the results are no longer the same. It's getting harder and harder to meet the targets you had aced with ease before.

It's possible you've been ignoring the issue for a while, hoping things will somehow work themselves out, but it's also been eating at you, and you can no longer stand it. You know you are kidding yourself. Things don't just fix themselves; you have to fix them.

People talk about diminishing returns, and now it's happening right there in your job. No wonder you are worried. You may be asking yourself questions like:

- What the heck is going on?
- What does this mean for the future?
- Should I be worried?
- What can I do differently?

I'm glad you found me, because I will tell you what's going on, and what you can do to fix it and get the wheel turning once again.

You can't rely on blind luck

Think your tried-and-true sales tactics are still cutting it? Think again. The B2B landscape isn't what it used to be—it's been flipped on its head thanks to digitalization, more informed buyers, and ever-evolving market dynamics. Given that is the case, how are you justifying your actions moving forward? Are you banking on intuition and gut feelings, or letting data guide your moves? Are your decisions grounded in evidence, or are they based on assumptions that were true five years ago but are now obsolete?

In today's hyper-competitive data-driven world, assumptions won't get you far.

Let me ask you this: how confident are you that your sales approach keeps pace with how businesses actually buy today? Do you know what's happening behind the scenes of your prospects' buying journey, or are you just hoping for the best?

Here's the harsh reality: guessing is dangerous in sales and marketing. What worked before can no longer be trusted blindly. It would be better to have facts—cold, hard numbers showing what's happening in B2B sales. The truth is, the buyer's journey has changed dramatically. Thanks to the internet, buyers are armed with more information than ever. They're doing their homework, coordinating internally, and involving more stakeholders in decision making. The old ways, where one or two decision makers called the shots, are long gone. It's a collective effort that demands a more strategic, research-driven sales approach.

You will fall behind if you still go on gut feelings and outdated strategies. If you let the data lead the way, you'll see the patterns, adapt to the trends, and stay ahead of the curve.

Stats that prove the shift in B2B sales

Ready to see just how much the game has changed? Let's dive into the numbers that prove it.

Eleven to twenty people or titles are involved in the buying process

Remember when it used to be just one decision maker in the room? When closing a deal meant winning over that one key contact with the golden handshake?

Those days are history.

Gaining B2B purchasing decisions is like trying to win over a jury—only the jury consists of eleven to twenty people, each with different role titles and priorities. Data shows that modern purchasing decisions involve various stakeholders from various departments—finance, procurement, IT, legal, operations, and marketing (Gartner, no date). This collaborative decision-making process reflects the complexity of today's business landscape. Every department has skin in the game, and each wants to ensure the purchase aligns with their specific goals and needs.

Why the change? Because in today's world, decisions are more expensive, complex, and risky. No one person wants the sole responsibility for signing off on a large purchase that could backfire. For this reason, companies spread the decision making across teams to mitigate risk and ensure all bases are covered.

Implication: What does this mean for your sales strategy? It's simple—you're no longer selling to one person. You're selling to a group, each individual with their own concerns, pain points, and priorities.

That means your pitch needs to be flexible, addressing the different needs of each player involved in the decision. Tailor your message to appeal to finance's obsession with cost efficiency, IT's concerns about integration, and legal's focus on compliance.

It's no longer about closing the deal—it's about satisfying the whole room.

22% of the customer's time is spent coordinating internally

Here's another surprising stat: B2B buyers spend 22% of their time coordinating internally before making a decision (Ellwood, 2017). That's nearly a quarter of the buying process dedicated to meetings, group emails, and Slack threads. Buyers are not negotiating with vendors but working out their internal priorities.

Think about what that means—during this critical time, buyers are focused on aligning their internal stakeholders, reconciling different opinions, setting budgets, and ensuring everyone's on the same page. No wonder deals can feel like they're dragging! Buyers aren't ghosting you—they're busy with internal bureaucracy.

Implication: Patience is your new best friend. Rather than push for immediate answers, understand that buyers need time to work through their internal processes. Your job is to equip them with the right resources and information so that when they finally do sit down to coordinate, your solution becomes the one that sticks in their minds.

Think of it like this: you're setting the table for the internal conversation, even if you're not in the room. The more prepared the buyers are with your insights and tools, the more likely it is they will advocate for your solution when the time comes.

45% of a buyer's time is spent on research

Remember when the salesperson was the fountain of all knowledge? Those days are long gone. Today's

B2B buyer is self-sufficient, spending a whopping 45% of their time researching independently (Gartner, no date) They're scouring your website, checking out your competitors, reading reviews, downloading white papers, and watching product demos—before they even think about picking up the phone. When a buyer finally reaches out to you, they already have a shortlist of options. They've formed strong opinions, maybe even made a decision.

This shift fundamentally changes the role of the salesperson. You're no longer the primary source of information—you're the closer.

Implication: Your digital presence is now your most important salesperson. You're invisible if your website, blog posts, case studies, and product pages aren't answering buyers' burning questions during their research phase. The conversation starts long before a sales rep gets involved. If your online resources are lacking, you've already lost the game. Think of your digital content as part of the buyer's journey, and make sure it's informative, persuasive, and easy to find.

80% of the buying process is over before the first contact

The days of early-stage conversations between buyers and salespeople are fading fast. Now, 80% of the purchasing journey is complete before a potential customer even reaches out to a supplier (6Sense, 2024).

They've researched their options, vetted suppliers, and created a shortlist by then.

In fact, a study by McKinsey & Company (2021) found that 75% of B2B buyers prefer digital self-service and remote engagement over face-to-face interactions. When they contact you, it's not to learn about your product—it's to finalize their decision.

Implication: Waiting for buyers to come to you is a recipe for irrelevance. You need to get ahead of the curve with a proactive approach. Invest in content marketing, search engine optimization (SEO), and targeted ads to ensure you're visible where buyers are doing their research. Your strategy must engage them long before they contact you, positioning you as the best option during their self-guided research phase.

Only 17% of purchasing time is spent talking to vendors

Here's another exciting clincher: out of the entire buying process, a mere 17% of the customer's time is spent talking to vendors (Gartner, no date). In other words, buyers aren't hanging on your every word—they're juggling various tasks, stakeholders, and information sources. When they finally engage with you, it's not for the typical sales pitch—they've done their homework, and they're simply looking for the last few pieces to complete their puzzle.

Implication: You've got a small window of opportunity, so make it count. Buyers don't want the hard sell; they want straight answers, clarity, and confidence. Focus on delivering sharp messaging that directly addresses their specific concerns. Listen carefully, offer tailored insights, and position yourself as the definitive solution to their problem.

Your value needs to be made crystal clear in that 17% of your prospects' time.

What's causing the difficulty in generating B2B sales?

I've mentioned that I've been in this marketing game for decades. In training several sales teams worldwide, I can safely say that I've kept pace with what's happening in the B2B space. Here's what I'll tell you: most people who struggle with generating sales in B2B are in that unfortunate situation for two main reasons:

- Overreliance on outdated sales methods

- A lack of a cohesive model

Sounds simplistic, doesn't it? Is it possible that these are the only issues that need fixing? Yes. Allow me to show you what I mean by that.

Overreliance on outdated sales methods

To understand why I say that many sales methods in B2B are outdated, it helps to look at how things have evolved over time.

For much of the last century, B2B sales were dominated by traditional relationship-driven methods. Sales representatives traveled far and wide to meet potential clients, build relationships, and close deals. The sales process was straightforward: cold calls led to face-to-face meetings, which led to negotiations, and finally, a handshake sealed the deal. It was a time when personal relationships and physical presence were the cornerstones of successful selling. In those days, information was a prized asset, often controlled by the salespeople. Prospects relied heavily on sales reps to provide insights into products and services. The salesperson was the gatekeeper of knowledge, and their ability to persuade and build trust was paramount. Cold calling, trade shows, and face-to-face meetings were the standard tools of the trade, and they worked. The sales process was linear, predictable, and often centered around long-term relationships.

However, as we have seen, the arrival of the internet marked the beginning of a seismic shift. Suddenly, information that was once scarce and guarded became abundant and easily accessible. Buyers no longer needed to rely solely on salespeople for information—they could find everything they needed with a quick search online. The balance of power began to shift from the seller to the buyer.

As technology continued to advance, the pace of change only quickened. Email, social media, and digital marketing transformed how businesses interacted with clients. The rise of online platforms meant buyers could research, compare, and evaluate options without speaking to a sales rep. B2B buyers became more self-sufficient, relying on digital content, online reviews, and peer recommendations to guide their decisions.

Today, most B2B buyers prefer to research online before purchasing. They value the ability to explore options, compare products, and read reviews independently, free from the influence of a sales pitch. Moreover, most of these buyers have already made up their minds before engaging with a sales rep. This digital-first behavior means that when potential customers reach out, they are often near the end of their decision-making journey.

The evolution of B2B sales from relationship-driven interactions to a digital-first approach has created a new reality where traditional tactics are no longer enough. The modern buyer is more informed, discerning, and demanding than ever. To thrive in this environment, you must adapt and evolve. You need to embrace the digital tools and strategies that can meet buyers where they are: online, informed, and ready to engage on their own terms.

Sound clear enough to you? Alright then, let's look at the other issue I find to be problematic.

A lack of a cohesive model

Look, I get it. You already have a model you rely on to generate sales for your company. Kudos for that. I respect it. In fact, we as marketers all need models to guide everything we do; otherwise, we might do nothing sustainable. Without a predictable business model, we don't generate $100 million in sales. It just doesn't happen.

The problem with many models that I've seen many sales and marketing executives develop in the companies I've consulted for is that they are superficial and ineffective. They lack thoroughness and substance, and many aren't adapted to the current B2B sales environment.

You see, you have to look at models like a map. A map helps you navigate a particular terrain. Suppose you wish to go from New York to Chicago. In that case, having the correct map of the relevant territory is key to getting where you want to go. Say someone gave you a map representing New York to Miami instead. Would that be a lot of help? Of course not. You could drive as fast as possible, but it wouldn't matter. You would only succeed in getting to the wrong place faster. So it is with many sales and marketing models today. They don't accurately mirror the environments they are designed to work in, and so they deliver poor results or even fail completely.

An effective model

Say you have a suitable model that accurately describes the territory you wish to navigate. In that case, stepping on the gas (deploying more marketing dollars) makes a huge difference.

That's what I'd like to address—to help you craft and adopt a model more befitting to the current B2B sales environment of the digital age.

Here's a representation of the model I'd like to talk about.

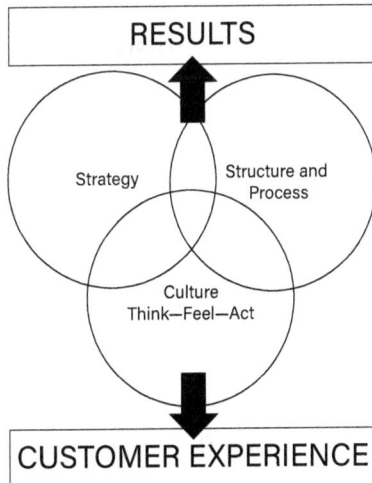

Strategic elements

> **Watch the video:** Go to https://
> salesmarketingmastery.com/video/
> strategic-elements or scan the
> QR code for insights and inspiration.

Let's discuss each element in greater detail.

Results

Virtually every B2B organization I've consulted for has an objective it aims for. It might be a goal to increase revenue, profit, or market share. That's all well and good, but do you know what the problem is? Results are not within anyone's direct control, no matter how good they are.

Imagine someone who's grossly out of shape. This person eats all the wrong foods and is a couch potato. The longest distance they ever walk is from the sofa to the fridge. This person admires in-shape people on the internet—healthy people with beautiful bodies that others want to emulate. Then they say to themselves: "I wish I had that." Would any of that help? Of course not.

What would?

According to Dr. Steven R. Covey, this person would do better to think of life issues in terms of the circle of control and circle of concern (Covey, 2013). Goals like having a great body or increasing your company's bottom line are in the circle of concern. You may have little actual control over these; they would take a vast amount of effort and commitment. Focusing your efforts and energies on your circle of concern only increases your feelings of frustration and inadequacy. You'll have more power over your life when you focus on your circle of control. For example, even if it is difficult for you to influence your exact body shape, you are in control of your diet and exercise. In other words, you would do yourself a world of good if you focused your efforts on things you can do something about fairly easily.

What's the most essential activity in the circle of control for most B2B organizations looking to improve their bottom line? It's simple, really. It's all about improving customer experience (CX).

Let's talk about that next.

CX

You've probably heard this statement: if you help others get what they want, you will get what you want. It's true, particularly in marketing. The more you focus on giving your customers the most incredible experience possible, the better off you'll be in business. It's a direct relationship. It's kinda like the golden goose from Aesop's fable. Your customers represent the golden goose. If you feed your goose well and take good care of it, you'll get a stable and reliable supply of golden eggs that will keep you happy over the long run, and you'll be successful. If you grow greedy and neglect the goose, its health will only deteriorate, and it might even die. Then, there will be no golden eggs coming anymore.

Put yourself in your customer's shoes. Look at the business from their point of view. How is their experience interacting with you? Does it suck? If it does, it's time to make some changes.

Ask yourself questions like:

- How good are we at approaching the market?

- How well is our website designed?

- Is our website easy to navigate and understand? Does it equal a smooth and seamless browsing experience?

- How effortless is the buying process?

- How good are we in offering after-sales services?

- How friendly and non-invasive are our marketing activities? Do they tend to piss people off?

Strategy

By strategy, I'm talking about the high-level plan that you and other executives in your company have put together to help you keep things in proper perspective. It's like having a bird's eye view of the territory you are operating in and the factors that should influence your success.

I love military analogies, so let me use one that puts things into perspective. Imagine that you are the President of the United States, and you've just made the decision to wage war against another country. You wouldn't just act willy-nilly. That would be reckless, and the outcome of such haphazard action would likely not be good. More than likely, you would invite the Joint Chiefs into the Oval Office and state your intentions and reasons for considering war. Then you would ask them to weigh in on the situation, going over the pros and cons, that kind of thing. You would look at the whole thing from a broader perspective to ensure you are not engaging in a foolish play.

That's the way it works in the corporate world as well. As a marketing executive, it's essential you ask yourself questions such as:

- What market are we operating in?
- Which segment of that market represents our ideal customers?
- What's the company's mission?
- What's the company's vision?

And so on.

However, strategy alone can never be enough. You also need structure and process. Let's talk about that now.

Structure and process

Having a bird's eye view of what you want and wish to achieve is good, but that's never enough, because you must return to earth and face the day-to-day realities of pursuing your objectives. How will you get the job done and in what sequence?

That's where structure and process come in. It's all about designing your company's internal operations to align with what you have in mind. This is analogous to being the brilliant military general who assembles a tactical playbook for carrying out missions and campaigns before going to the battlefield.

Ask yourself how well the sales process in your business is optimized from end to end. Not only that, but how well does this process match up with a typical buyer's journey?

I say that because a problem I often see in many companies I consult with is that the sales people, the marketing people, and the after-sales people are operating independently in silos, doing their own thing. That's wrong because it creates a disjointed situation that hurts the CX. When dealing with the company, a prospect often feels like they are dealing with different organizations, each unaware of what the others are doing. Rather than work hard to understand all this mess, the prospect gives up and looks elsewhere.

To avoid this unfortunate scenario, it's important that all three departments merge their efforts and work toward a common goal.

Culture

Finally, I wanna bring in the last piece of the puzzle, and that's culture. When discussing culture, I refer to behavior, work habits, attitudes, motivation, skills, etc. In other words, how do the people in your team think, feel, and act toward the market and internally? It might not seem like a big deal, but culture affects how your company interacts with the market, which creates the most significant impact on CX.

The best way I know of putting this into perspective is to take you back to the events of World War II. Everyone knows how the Nazis terrorized Europe before deciding to launch an attack on Britain. The Germans thought they had air superiority and could bully Britain to its knees through bombing raids. Hermann Göring—the man in charge of the air defense forces in Germany—told Hitler that the mission was as good as accomplished before it even started.

He was wrong.

The Britons fought the Nazis, who started to back down for the first time since the war had begun due to an overwhelming number of casualties. Have you ever wondered why the British pilots fought so bravely?

The answer was primarily culture.

I've heard that Göring's defense pilots finished their trips and returned home to Germany exhausted, only to have to deliver comprehensive reports on what had gone wrong in battle and what could be made better. They were accorded no special treatment whatsoever. In Britain, things were different. Defense pilots were seen more as heroes than anything else. They could finish their runs, go to bars, and get free beer and food. In other words, they were treated essentially as first-class citizens. Do you think that helped morale? Of course, it did. In Germany, people in the armed forces felt more like cogs in a wheel. In Britain, they felt they mattered—their country appreciated and honored their sacrifice. In return, they fought like hell.

That's how big a difference culture can make, whether it's in the military or the sales department of a B2B organization.

THE GAME HAS CHANGED

The sweet spot—creating synergy

When you have strategy, structure and process, and culture working together, in the center of the model, you have synergy. It's kinda like a high-performance engine.

Strategy is the engine's design—the blueprint that outlines how everything should work together to achieve maximum efficiency. It drives where the car is going and how fast it can get there. Structure and process are the individual parts of the engine—the gears, pistons, and belts—that must be precisely aligned and operating in sync for it to run smoothly. Without a robust structure and well-oiled processes, even the best engine design will sputter and stall.

Then there's culture, the fuel that powers the engine. Culture provides the energy, the enthusiasm, and the drive. It's what keeps the engine running at peak performance. A positive, high-octane culture in business ensures that the team is motivated, engaged, and aligned with the company's goals, just as premium fuel ensures a car's engine runs smoothly without knocking or stalling.

When all three elements—strategy, structure and process, and culture—work together, you have an engine that fires on all cylinders. Like a well-tuned engine, a B2B sales model built on these three pillars accelerates performance, outpaces the competition, and easily navigates the road to success. It propels the sales machine forward, driving revenues, boosting profits, and increasing market share.

This synergy creates momentum to turn a good company into a great one. It's the difference between merely getting by and thriving in today's competitive B2B landscape.

2
The Core Factors

What if I told you that most sales teams fail because they miss one critical element? Just one.

Maybe you've got the best people on your team—top talent, sharp as knives. You've invested in the latest tech, all the gadgets, and the software that promises to take you to the next level. You've even laid out the goals and given pep talks that would make a football coach proud. Despite all that, things aren't clicking. Sales are flat. Leads trickle in slower than you'd like. Every month, you're left scratching your head, wondering, "What am I missing?"

Ever stop to consider it's not the hustle that's the problem? Maybe it's something bigger. Something fundamental.

Could your team be missing one of the four critical factors that make all the difference between hitting those targets and always falling short?

What you really need

Here's the thing: to build a sales and marketing team that delivers results, it's not enough to just hustle. Hustle is excellent—don't get me wrong—but without direction, all that effort can feel like running on a treadmill. You're moving, but you're not getting anywhere. What you really need is a strategy. Not just any strategy, but one grounded in four core factors.

These aren't just fancy buzzwords. They're the backbone of any team that is consistently knocking it out of the park. If you're missing even one core factor, you're basically trying to build a house without a foundation.

Think about it. You wouldn't skip the foundation when building your dream home and expect it to stand tall, would you? The same goes for your sales and marketing team. Miss a core factor, and you're setting yourself up for cracks, collapses, and… disaster.

What are these four core factors?

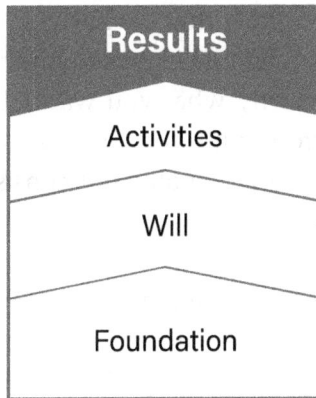

Measurement objectives

Let's break down the core factors.

Results

You must ask yourself a simple question: "What's the finish line here?" Every company leader has some idea of the prize they're chasing—revenue, profits, market share—but vague aspirations don't cut it. Are you crystal clear on your specific goals?

Let's say you want to increase revenue—OK, but how much? Are you gunning for a 10% bump this quarter, or are you eyeing a more aggressive 25% leap over the year?

Maybe it's market share. Great, but again I ask, how much? Are you aiming to capture 5% of the market within twelve months?

Then there's profit. If that's what you target, what's the figure? How can you expect to hit the target without knowing exactly what you want? It's like trying to shoot an arrow with your eyes closed. Sure, you might get lucky occasionally, but consistent success? Forget about it.

You've got to set concrete measurable goals. It's not just about saying, "We want to grow." It's about defining that growth precisely, giving your team a clear target to rally around. Otherwise, you're just tossing darts in the dark and hoping something sticks.

Activities

What are your people really doing day in and day out? It's easy to get lost in the illusion of productivity—endless meetings, cold calls, emails flying back and forth—but are these actions actually moving the needle? You've got to ask yourself: "Are our salespeople focusing on the high-impact activities that drive results?"

The right actions, done consistently, can be the difference between smashing targets and simply treading water. Maybe it's strategic outreach, building relationships with key decision makers, or refining the sales pitch until it's irresistible that is key for your team. The problem is, too often, teams get bogged down with low-value tasks. They're busy, sure, but are they being productive? If they're not, it's like a hamster on a wheel, running and running, and getting nowhere.

It would be best to define the key activities to propel the business forward and ensure your team spends time there, not drowning in distractions. Focus on what matters. That's how results are made.

Will

Without the will to succeed, your team's dead in the water. You can have the sharpest strategy, slickest tools, and best-laid plans, but nothing will happen if your salespeople aren't fired up. Not a thing.

What drives them? Is it money? Recognition? Career growth? Maybe it's the sheer thrill of the win. Here's a crazy truth about motivation: it's not a one-size-fits-all thing. You're missing a huge part of the puzzle if you don't know what fuels each individual on your team.

Think of it this way: even the fastest car in the world won't go anywhere without gas. For your sales team, will is that fuel. If you're not regularly tapping into their motivations—personal or professional—you'll end up with a group of people just going through the motions. They'll show up and put in the hours, but they won't own it.

When they're not personally invested, no amount of strategy or structure will push your team members to go that extra mile. You've got to figure out what lights their fire and then keep that flame alive. Without it? You might as well park the Ferrari in the garage.

Foundation

The people on your team are only as strong as the resources backing them. In this case, I'm not just talking about tools (such as software). I'm also referring to skills. Yes, skills are resources too—intangible ones. They are the kind that can make or break your sales efforts. You see, if your team members don't have the right blend of product knowledge, market insights, and negotiation skills, it's almost like asking them to climb Everest in flip-flops.

Ask yourself: "Do our people know their way around tools like customer relationship management systems (CRMs)? Is their market knowledge sharp and up-to-date? Are they equipped with the product insights they need to sound credible and win over prospects?"

These are crucial elements to consider if you want your team to succeed. Because if they're trying to sell without the right skills, your people might as well be flying blind, and we both know where that leads—missed targets, frustrated team members, and countless lost opportunities. That's why you need to build a solid foundation of skills and training, not just invest in the latest tech. It's about ensuring your team feels confident using the tools, has seamless systems to rely on, and possesses the skills to handle any prospect interaction effectively.

Remember, this foundation is what holds everything together. Without the right skills and resources, your strategy will crumble, your activities will falter, and your team's motivation will quickly dry up. You can't let that happen.

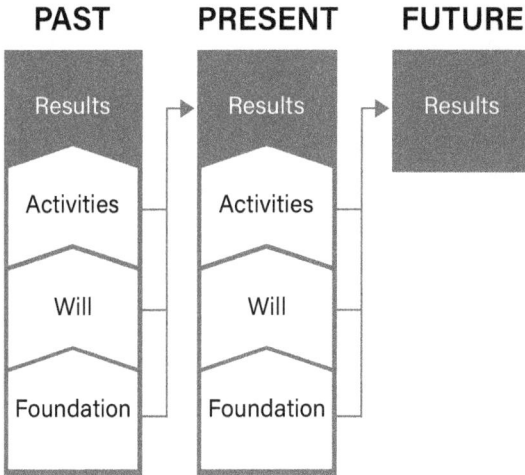

Balanced management by objective

Watch the video: Got to https://salesmarketingmastery.com/video/balanced-mbo-future or scan the QR code for insights and inspiration.

3
External Vs.
Internal Factors

Why do some companies soar while others crash and burn? Is it pure genius, some secret sauce locked inside their internal structure? Could it be that forces outside their walls—forces they can't control—are steering the ship?

Here's an even more challenging question: do you give yourself a pat on the back when your sales are skyrocketing? Of course, you do. You're the mastermind behind it all, but what happens when the numbers tank? Do you still stand tall or do you point fingers at the economy, ruthless competitors, or that elusive 'state of the market'?

Be honest—how often do you chalk up success to your company's brilliance but blame external forces when things go wrong? It's like running a race and claiming victory thanks to your training, but if you lose? The weather was terrible, the track was uneven, or your competitors had an unfair advantage.

Here's the hard truth: real long-term success isn't just about what's going on inside your business; it's about how seamlessly you align your internal factors with the external ones.

Think of it like this: your company is a ship, and the sea is the external world. You can have the strongest crew, the best captain, and the most state-of-the-art navigation system, but if you can't read the waves or adapt to the wind, your ship is going nowhere—or worse, it'll sink. Too often, when businesses are riding high, their leaders pop champagne and toast to their internal brilliance—their strategic genius, flawless processes, and bulletproof culture. When the tide turns and the ship starts taking on water, it's suddenly not their fault. "The market's too competitive." "The economy's in the tank." "Our customers' needs are changing."

Here's the catch: blaming external factors when you fail and ignoring them when you succeed is a sure way to capsize your business. The real secret to success is mastering both sides of the equation. You can't control the storm, but you can build a ship that won't sink—and that's where the alignment of internal and external factors comes in. Mastering the balance between what's inside and outside is the key to staying afloat no matter how rough the waters get.

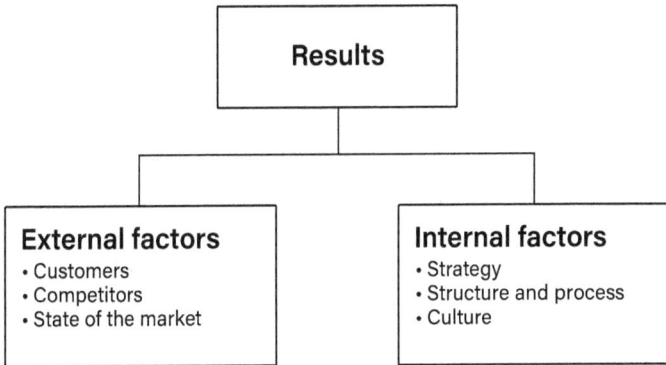

```
                    ┌─────────────────┐
                    │     Results     │
                    └─────────────────┘
              ┌──────────────┴──────────────┐
┌─────────────────────────┐   ┌─────────────────────────┐
│ External factors         │   │ Internal factors         │
│ • Customers              │   │ • Strategy               │
│ • Competitors            │   │ • Structure and process  │
│ • State of the market    │   │ • Culture                │
└─────────────────────────┘   └─────────────────────────┘
```

External and internal factors

Watch the video: Go to https:// salesmarketingmastery.com/video/ external-internal-factors or scan the QR code for insights and inspiration.

Let's examine both external and internal factors in greater depth.

External factors

These forces exist outside your company's control. They're the variables that shape your market, your competition, and your customers' evolving needs. You can't dictate them—you can only respond to them intelligently.

Let's return to the ship analogy. These external factors are the weather you're sailing through. Some days, it's sunny, calm, and perfect for smooth sailing. Other days? Then, it's a full-blown storm. You can't stop the storm, but how well you've prepared your ship determines whether you'll navigate it or get swept away.

The most significant external factors that drive results include the following.

Customers

Who are they? What do they need? Perhaps the most critical question is, how are their behaviors and preferences shifting over time?

Your customers are the lifeblood of your business. Without them, you're dead in the water, but the catch is: you can't force them to buy. You can only persuade them by deeply understanding their needs, pain points, and desires. Are you actively listening to your customers? Are you adapting to their evolving needs or sticking with what worked last year, hoping it'll work again?

Competitors

Every industry has rivals vying for the same slice of the pie. What's the harsh reality regarding them? You can't control what your competitors do. You can't stop them from launching new products, undercutting your prices, or wooing your customers away. The magic happens only when you can control how you respond.

Are you watching their every move? Are you learning from their successes and capitalizing on their failures? Are you seizing opportunities they've missed or ignoring them while they quietly steal market share?

State of the market

The economy, industry trends, and government regulations play a massive role in your company's success. These factors are outside your control, but how well are you navigating these unpredictable waters? Are you agile enough to pivot and adjust your strategy when the economy takes a nosedive? Are you aware of the emerging trends that could disrupt your industry, or are you too focused on what's in front of you to see the wave coming?

The ability to read the market and make timely adjustments is often the difference between thriving and merely surviving.

Internal factors

You can control these elements—the internal mechanisms fueling your business. Think of them as the engine that powers your organization. Like any engine, your internal factors require constant maintenance and fine-tuning to keep pace with the external forces. The stronger and more efficient your internal factors, the better you can respond to the challenges outside your walls.

Here are the core internal factors.

Strategy

Your strategy is your game plan, the blueprint for how you will succeed in the current environment. The question is: are you setting clear, actionable goals that align with the external landscape, or are you still relying on outdated assumptions and yesterday's tactics?

In a constantly shifting market, a flexible, well-thought-out strategy is essential. It's the difference between leading the pack or playing catch-up. Your strategy has to be both long-term and adaptable—designed to get you where you want to go, but agile enough to shift when the external winds change direction.

Structure and process

Structure and process are like the scaffolding that supports your strategy. You can have the most brilliant game plan in the world, but without the proper structure and processes, it's all just a dream.

How well is your company organized to achieve its goals? Is your sales team structured for maximum efficiency? Are there processes to ensure that the right actions happen at the right time, every time?

When things get busy, a solid process is what prevents chaos. It's the invisible hand guiding your team toward consistent execution, without which even the best strategy will crumble.

Culture

Culture is the soul of your company. It's the collective mindset, the values, the unwritten rules that shape how your team operates.

Is your culture one that motivates and drives success, or is it breeding complacency and disengagement? A motivated, well-aligned team will take your strategy and run with it, but one with a toxic or unmotivated culture? That's like trying to drive with the parking brake on—it slows everything down.

The best leaders know that success doesn't just come from smart strategies and efficient processes, but also from cultivating a culture where people are inspired to bring their best selves to work daily.

AN EXAMPLE: The CEO at the reunion

Let's end this chapter with a real-world example of what we've covered. Imagine this: a CEO who is on top of the world. Sales are skyrocketing in their company, profits are strong, and they're the center of attention at their high school reunion.

Everyone's asking, "What's your secret?" The CEO beams with pride and explains how they built an elite team, developed a flawless strategy, and fostered a top-notch company culture. In their mind, it's clear— they created a well-oiled machine, and success was inevitable.

Fast forward to the next reunion, a year later. The company's hit a rough patch. Sales are down, profits are thin, and the mood is somber. The CEO is still getting questions, but this time, it's, "What went wrong?"

The answer? Suddenly, it's not about internal factors anymore.

"The market tanked," they say. "Competition got brutal, and customers are acting unpredictably."

What's the truth in the example above? Sure, the market shifted, competitors may have gotten more aggressive, and customers' needs likely are changing, but the real issue? The CEO didn't adapt things within their company. Their internal factors—strategy, structure, and culture—stayed static while their external world changed. Instead of pivoting when the market shifted, they doubled down on the same old game plan, letting external factors outpace them. It wasn't bad luck; it was the company's failure to align internal strengths with external realities.

The key takeaway? Success isn't just about what's happening inside the company; failure isn't purely about external forces.

How well a company adapts the internal to match the external separates the winners from the losers.

4
The Customer Journey

Remember the days when the salesperson held all the power? When they were the gatekeepers of knowledge, and buyers came to them for the answers? When a simple conversation could seal the deal, and information was a scarce commodity, doled out at the salesperson's discretion? As we have already discussed, those days are long gone. Today, buyers are not just informed; they're almost omniscient. They have the world's knowledge at their fingertips and are more skeptical, empowered, and selective than ever before.

How does your B2B sales strategy stack up in this new era of digitalization? Are you still clinging to outdated methods, or have you adapted to the fact that the game's rules have changed?

B2B sales have experienced seismic shifts in the digital age. The way we sell and the way buyers buy have been fundamentally transformed. What worked in the past—when salespeople were the primary source of information, and the sales cycle was linear—is no longer effective. Today, buyers are in control. They've done their research, compared options, and often made up their minds long before they even engage with your sales team.

According to a report by Forrester Research (2021), over 70% of the B2B buyer's journey is completed before they even speak to a sales representative. Your sales strategy must reflect this new reality. If your approach still revolves around the old methods—where the salesperson is the hero and information is a privilege to be granted—you're at a significant disadvantage. To stay relevant and competitive, your strategy must embrace the changes in digitalization. This means understanding how the sales process has evolved and adjusting your approach to meet the new expectations of informed, empowered buyers.

The four phases of industrialization

Let's break down how this transformation occurred by exploring the evolution of sales through the four phases of industrialization.

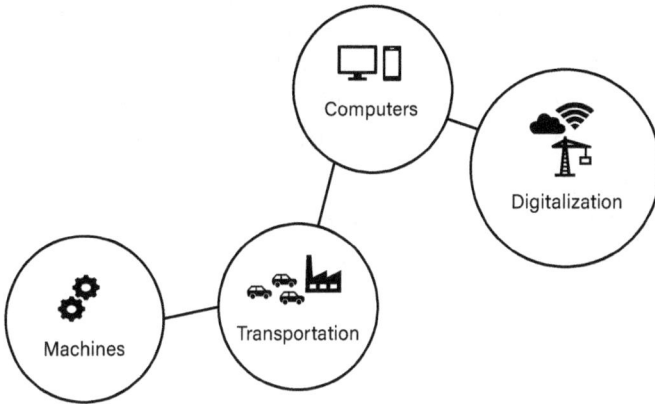

The four industrial revolutions

Watch the video: Go to https://
salesmarketingmastery.com/video/
industrial-revolutions or scan the
QR code for insights and inspiration.

Machines: The steam engine era

The dawn of industrialization was marked by the invention of machines like the steam engine, which revolutionized manufacturing and transportation. This era was where innovation was tangible and transformative—iron wheels turned, steam-powered engines roared, and products began moving faster and further than ever before.

B2B SALES AND MARKETING MASTERY

In this world, sales were deeply rooted in local networks. Businesses succeeded by establishing strong connections within their immediate surroundings and maintaining a tight grip on their territory. Salespeople during this era were the go-to experts. They had the information that buyers needed because access to knowledge was limited. Buyers often had no choice but to rely on these salespeople as their primary sources of information.

This exclusivity gave salespeople a position of power and trust. They were not just vendors; they were the custodians of knowledge. If you wanted to make a purchase, you went through them, and the information they provided was your only window into the market.

Transportation: The age of mobility

The transportation revolution changed everything. The world became smaller with the advent of motor vehicles, trains, and ships. This new mobility allowed salespeople to extend their reach beyond local markets, making connections with customers in distant regions possible. Sales territories grew, and businesses could tap into new and diverse markets.

Despite the broader reach, buyers still found themselves dependent on salespeople. The sheer variety of products and the complexities of choosing among them required guidance. Salespeople became the navigators of this expanded marketplace, helping customers make sense of their options and guiding them through the decision-making process.

While buyers had more choices and could access products from afar, the salesperson's expertise and personalized advice remained crucial in helping them through their purchasing decisions.

Computers: The information revolution

The advent of computers was a seismic shift for every industry. Suddenly, businesses could operate on a global scale. Communication became instantaneous, and data flowed more freely than ever before.

This new era of information accessibility began to reshape the sales and marketing landscape. Yet, despite the wealth of data and improved communication, salespeople continued to hold the reins. While buyers now had more access to information, they still turned to sales teams to help them navigate the technical details and complexities of products and services. Salespeople were the experts who could provide insights and answer questions that went beyond the raw data. Their role was essential in interpreting information, offering personalized advice, and ensuring customers made informed decisions.

In this era, salespeople remained pivotal, even as the tools of their trade evolved.

Digitalization: The age of the internet

Welcome to the digital era—the game-changer transforming the sales landscape in ways many of us struggle with.

The internet arrived like a tidal wave, bringing information to buyers' fingertips. Without relying on salespeople to provide answers, buyers can now conduct their own research, compare options, and make informed decisions before picking up the phone. According to Gartner (no date), the time buyers spend interacting with sales reps has decreased significantly, as they prefer to conduct research independently online. In this age of digitalization, the power dynamic has flipped. Buyers are in control. They drive the conversations, set the pace, and choose how and when to engage with your company.

Salespeople, once the gatekeepers of knowledge, now find themselves in a new role—one where they must adapt to the buyer's journey and offer value in a landscape where information is abundant and easily accessible. To thrive in this environment, sales strategies must evolve, focusing on adding value, building relationships, and meeting buyers where they are in their decision-making process.

Here's yet another element to include in your strategic playbook. How will you adapt to the current digitalized world, where salespeople no longer have the power they once had?

What you need to do

Have you considered what happens between the first time a prospect hears about your brand and when they become one of your most loyal customers? What triggers them to move from casual awareness to "I have to buy this"? Why do they decide to stick with you and not move to your competition?

The customer journey doesn't start when they click buy, nor does it end with a sale. It's a complex, winding path that involves multiple touchpoints, decisions, emotions, and moments of hesitation.

Are you paying attention to every stage of this process, or are you laser-focused on closing the deal and missing crucial opportunities to deepen your relationships? Here's the thing: the companies that win in today's B2B landscape aren't just the ones with the best products—they're the ones that understand their customers' journey. They engage early, offer help when it's needed most, and continue building trust long after the sale.

As journalist and author Malcolm Gladwell (2000) discusses in his book *The Tipping Point*, small, seemingly insignificant interactions can accumulate and create a major impact on a customer's decision-making process. A good strategy doesn't just aim to close the sale; it's about understanding and optimizing the entire customer journey—from their initial discovery of your brand to you fostering long-term loyalty.

Each phase of this journey represents a critical opportunity for your business to connect, build trust, and deliver value. If you're only focused on the final sale, you're leaving a lot of untapped potential on the table.

The customer journey can be broken down into distinct phases with challenges and opportunities. By understanding these phases, you can guide your prospects and customers with more purpose, ensuring that your marketing, sales, and post-purchase efforts work harmoniously to create a seamless experience. As leading marketing thinkers Philip Kotler and Kevin Lane Keller emphasize in their book *Marketing Management* (2019), understanding the customer's path is critical for delivering value at every stage of the buying process.

Let's dig into these phases, step by step, to uncover where your strategy can have the most impact.

Watch the video: Go to https://salesmarketingmastery.com/video/infinity-loop or scan the QR code for insight and inspiration.

The customer journey breakdown

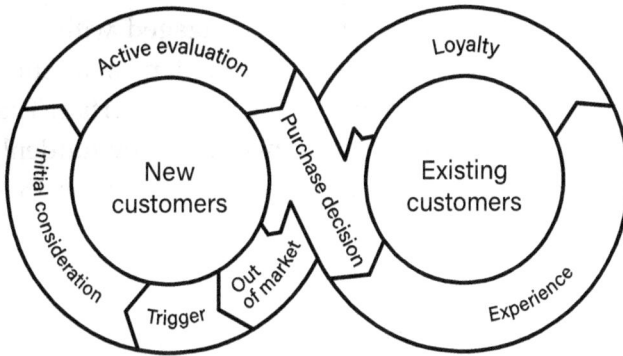

The infinity loop customer journey

Out of market

At any given moment, most of your potential buyers aren't in the market for what you're selling. They do not immediately need your product or service and aren't even considering purchasing. Take, for example, a manufacturing plant with a fleet of trucks running smoothly. The trucks are in perfect condition, doing their job day in and day out. The plant manager isn't browsing truck dealerships or having meetings about replacements. They're not interested—yet.

Implication: This is where many companies make a crucial mistake: they overlook prospects who aren't ready to buy. Just because prospects aren't currently in the market doesn't mean they won't be in the future.

Your goal here isn't to push for a sale, but to plant the seed. Keep these prospects engaged with your brand in subtle, helpful ways—content marketing, emails, or even ads highlighting your expertise. That way, when their situation changes and they suddenly need what you offer, guess who's already on their radar? You.

Trigger

Then, something shifts. A trigger event—a catalyst that sparks the prospect to reconsider their current situation—brings them into the market.

Let's stick with the manufacturing plant example. After five years of heavy use, the once-reliable fleet of trucks is starting to show signs of wear and tear. Maintenance costs are rising, and breakdowns are becoming more frequent. The plant manager now has a reason to reconsider the status quo. Suddenly, replacing the trucks is back on the table.

Implication: When a prospect experiences a trigger event, they begin looking for answers. This is your first real opportunity to move the needle.

The key is to anticipate these trigger points and be prepared. Whether it's content that educates prospects on the benefits of newer models or personalized outreach, your strategy should focus on guiding them through the initial stages of exploring solutions—your solutions. You need to be ready with timely, relevant, and valuable information that leads them to consider your offerings as a natural next step.

Initial consideration

Once triggered, the prospect starts to explore their initial options. This is where they weigh the pros and cons of addressing the problem head-on.

Let's go back to the plant manager. After realizing the trucks are wearing out, the manager starts doing mental math. Is it worth the cost of procuring new trucks, or is it more cost-effective to squeeze a few more years out of the old ones? This is when they ask, "Is this a problem I need to solve now, or can it wait?"

Implication: This is where you need to make your value proposition crystal clear. At this stage, buyers are assembling a shortlist of potential solutions. They're forming their initial opinions based on how well your offering addresses their needs versus sticking with the status quo. You want to ensure that you are part of that initial consideration set and that your solution stands out as the most attractive option. Your messaging should highlight why acting now with your product or service is the best decision your prospect could make.

Active evaluation

Now things get interesting. Having moved beyond just considering options, the buyer starts actively researching and comparing alternatives. For instance, that plant manager who initially focused on the cost of new diesel trucks may now be reading about environmental regulations or future tax hikes on diesel vehicles. Suddenly, they consider electric trucks as a potentially smarter long-term investment. They're evaluating every option on the table and factoring in new angles they hadn't considered.

Implication: This is the critical phase where your content marketing needs to work overtime. Your blog posts, case studies, white papers, and product comparisons should guide the buyer's thought process. This isn't just about making your product look good; it's about framing the conversation around the key challenges and showing why your solution is the best fit. Thought leadership becomes crucial here.

Suppose you're educating buyers, positioning your company as a knowledgeable, forward-thinking partner. In that case, you're not just selling a product—you're shaping how they understand the problem and the range of solutions available.

Purchase decision

After all the evaluation, comparison, and internal discussions, the buyer reaches a pivotal moment—the decision to buy. At this point, they've likely narrowed their options to a shortlist, and now it's time for them to choose. For the plant manager, that might mean finally purchasing those electric trucks after weighing all the pros and cons.

This is where you step in and close the deal. The buyer has done their research, and they need tailored guidance to make the final commitment.

Implication: Your job here is to make the decision-making process as smooth as possible. Avoid complicating things with convoluted pricing, hidden terms, or confusing offers. Be transparent about contract terms and align them with the buyer's needs.

This is not the time for a hard sell, but for reassurance. You want to eliminate any last-minute doubts and make it effortless for the buyer to say yes to your offer. At this stage, you're not just closing a sale—you're closing the loop on trust and delivering a solution.

Experience

Once the sale is complete, the customer's journey doesn't end—it's only just beginning. Now it's time to deliver on the promises you made. Whether it's through onboarding assistance, providing how-to guides, offering customer support, or even recommending complementary services, your role is to ensure that the customer gets the most value from what they've purchased.

For instance, the plant manager who bought your electric trucks will need to know how to integrate them into the existing fleet, train employees on their use, and troubleshoot any issues.

Implication: A great post-purchase experience is critical to ensuring customer satisfaction and long-term success. It's not enough to make the sale—you must follow through and help customers feel confident in their decision.

Proactive support—like check-ins, resource sharing, or offering upgrades—builds trust and strengthens your relationship with the customer. When customers feel supported and see the tangible benefits of their purchase, you lay the groundwork for loyalty.

Loyalty

Customers who see consistent value in your product or service begin to trust you, which transforms into loyalty. Loyal customers are invaluable—they're not just repeat buyers; they become advocates for your brand.

Picture that plant manager who swears by your electric trucks and tells colleagues in other plants about how your solution transformed their operations. These loyal customers will actively recommend your brand, driving new business without you lifting a finger.

Implication: Building loyalty goes beyond delivering a functional product; it's about fostering a relationship. Create personalized touchpoints that make customers feel valued, such as recognizing milestones, offering special perks, or spotlighting their successes. Let your customers feel like they're part of your brand's story, and they'll be more likely to stick around—and spread the word.

The cycle begins again

Eventually, the time will come when your existing customers need a new solution or a replacement for what they already have. Who are they likely to turn to first? You—if you've nurtured the relationship effectively. This repeat business is a testament to the trust and value you've built over time.

Implication: The customer journey doesn't end with the sale; it's a continuous loop. By consistently delivering value and maintaining solid relationships, you increase the likelihood that your customers will return to you when they need more. This cycle of repeat business transforms good companies into great ones, creating a steady stream of loyal customers who keep returning.

The buying journey

Look, I'll be the first one to admit that the traditional customer journey feels a bit too overwhelming, so let's look at a more condensed version that helps keep things in proper perspective. I call it the buying journey.

It consists of three critical steps:

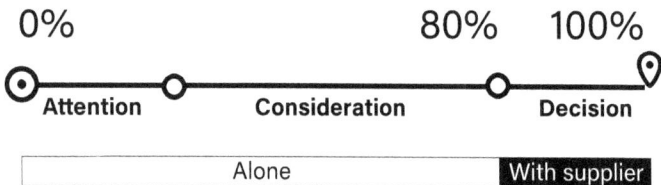

The buying journey

Watch the video: Go to https://salesmarketingmastery.com/video/customer-journey or scan the QR code for insights and inspiration.

Attention

This is where the buyer's journey begins. They become aware of a potential need to purchase after a trigger event, but at this stage, no decisions have been made, and they likely aren't even talking to a salesperson. They're just gathering information and exploring their options.

Implication: At this stage, your digital content is doing the heavy lifting. Buyers are researching independently through your website, social media, blogs, and other resources. You're influencing them, but indirectly. Make sure you're present where they're looking—on Google, LinkedIn, industry-specific forums, and other digital platforms—so you can capture their attention early and establish your brand as a key player.

Consideration

Here, the customer starts doing more serious research. They're comparing options, reading reviews, and discussing internally. They might also seek recommendations and input from others in the industry or market.

Implication: Consideration represents about 80% of the buying journey. At this stage, you're still not likely to hear from the prospect directly. Your role here is crucial: ensure your online content, case studies, and social proof (like testimonials) are robust and easily accessible. You risk being overlooked if your brand isn't visible or compelling during the consideration phase. Proactively provide valuable, engaging content that keeps you top-of-mind as the prospect evaluates their options.

Decision

This is where the buyer is ready to make a final decision. They've narrowed their options and are now engaging with salespeople to clarify details, finalize terms, and seal the deal.

Implication: The decision phase represents the final 10% of the buying journey. At this stage, you need to make every interaction count. Buyers seek clear, concise answers and solutions that address their needs. You aim to simplify decision making and provide outstanding support to close the deal. Since buyers have already done most of their research, your role is to reinforce their choice and facilitate a smooth, confident purchase experience.

The customer journey is a complex cyclical process that requires B2B companies to engage at every stage—from the initial spark of interest to long after the first sale. Those who understand the journey and support customers through it are the ones who build lasting, profitable relationships.

5
Change In Buyer Behavior

Have you felt the seismic shift in buyer behavior recently? Does it seem like your once-reliable strategies are now missing the mark? Why are buyers increasingly avoiding direct interactions with sales reps, and how is the explosion of online purchasing reshaping your approach? What do you do when prospects are drowning in a sea of information and struggling to make decisions? Are you tuned in to the true fears and motivations driving your prospects in a landscape where every choice feels monumental?

In today's rapidly evolving B2B landscape, adapting to changing buyer behavior is not just beneficial, it's essential. Buyers are now spending more time conducting independent research, influenced by the acceleration of digitalization and an overwhelming influx of information. The traditional fear of missing out (FOMO) has shifted to a more critical concern: the fear of making the wrong decision, or fear of messing up (FOMU). This shift from FOMO to FOMU reflects a growing emphasis on risk aversion in purchasing decisions (Adamson and Dixon, 2013). To remain competitive, you need to understand and address this shift.

This chapter will delve into how these changes affect your strategy and offer actionable insights to help you navigate and succeed in this new era of buyer behavior.

In what ways have buyers changed?

B2B customers' buying behavior is changing owing to several factors:

- More time without sales reps
- Accelerated digitization
- Information overload

Let's look at each in more detail.

More time without sales reps

In today's market, buyers are increasingly spend-ing time researching and making decisions without the direct involvement of sales representatives. This change is driven by the vastness of online resources and a growing preference for self-guided exploration. Prospects are now accustomed to finding information, comparing options, and evaluating solutions on their own, often before reaching out to a sales team.

Implication: To adapt, your strategy must prioritize enhancing your digital presence. Focus on creating and curating valuable content that helps guide prospects through their journey independently. This means investing in high-quality resources like detailed product information, educational blogs, and helpful case studies that can lead prospects toward your solutions without the need for direct interaction.

Accelerated digitalization

The surge in online purchasing has transformed how transactions occur. Buyers are now comfortable researching, comparing, and completing massive online purchases.

The digital landscape has become the primary arena for many business interactions, making it crucial for companies to meet prospects where they are—online.

Implication: Adopt and integrate digital tools and platforms into your engagement strategy. Ensure your online resources are not only comprehensive, but also accessible and user-friendly. This includes having an intuitive website, effective SEO practices, and leveraging online channels to engage with prospects in their digital space.

Information overload

Prospects today are overwhelmed with a torrent of information from multiple sources. This flood of data can lead to decision paralysis, where the sheer volume of content means it's difficult for buyers to make informed choices.

Implication: Information overload isn't necessarily a bad thing—it's an opportunity. With so much information out there, your prospects are overwhelmed and looking for someone who can cut through the clutter. This is your chance to stop selling and start making it easy for people to buy.

No one wants to feel like they're being pushed into a decision. Instead, they want to feel like they're making the right choice on their own terms. Your messaging needs to be clear, concise, and focused on helping customers make the best decision for their needs. Instead of bombarding them with more data, simplify the information and guide them toward the solution that fits best. By positioning your team as trusted advisors who help customers navigate their options, you shift the dynamic from selling to helping them buy.

Your job is to distill complex information into easily digestible formats that highlight the core value of your offering, empowering the customer to make an informed choice they feel great about. In a world full of noise, your clarity and focus on the customer's needs become your competitive edge. You're not just another salesperson—they see you as a partner who's there to help them make the right call.

FOMO vs. FOMU

Historically, FOMO was a significant driver in buyer behavior. Prospects used to worry about missing out on valuable deals, opportunities, or exclusive offers. However, in today's environment, this has shifted toward FOMU—the fear of investing in a solution that fails to deliver the promised results. Buyers are now more concerned with the potential consequences of making a wrong decision, such as financial loss, operational setbacks, or reputational damage.

Implication: Your strategy must build buyer confidence in your solution to address this evolved fear effectively. It's essential to demonstrate how you mitigate risks and ensure value. Instead of merely emphasizing the opportunities buyers might miss out on, provide clear evidence of how your solution will meet their needs and deliver the expected outcomes. This might include showcasing success stories, offering guarantees, and detailing your approach to customer support and follow-up.

Addressing FOMU can build trust and improve your chances of closing the sale.

Where's the evidence?

Let's look at some key facts about decision making and their implications for B2B sales (Dixon, 2022):

- **85% of all sales conversations in B2B have medium to high levels of indecision.** Imagine navigating a maze where every turn presents a new dilemma. That's the reality for many buyers today. A staggering 85% of sales conversations in B2B are marked by significant indecision (Miller, 2024). Buyers are overwhelmed by the complexity of their choices, each weighing heavily on their minds. They are not just worried about choosing a product or service; they think about making a decision that will profoundly impact their business.

- **40–60% of all deals end up stalled in no-decision limbo.** Picture this: after numerous discussions, presentations, and evaluations, many deals come to a screeching halt. Between 40% and 60% of deals get stuck in no-decision limbo (Dixon and McKenna, 2022). This is where momentum dies, and the deal stalls in uncertainty. Buyers are caught in indecision and cannot commit to a final choice.

- **56% of no decisions stem from an inability to make a decision.** More than half of these no decisions are not due to a failure on the part of buyers to recognize the offer's value. Instead, they stem from the buyers' struggle to make clear decisions (Dixon and McKenna, 2022). It's not that they don't see the benefits; they can't overcome the internal barriers that prevent them from choosing.

Implication: Your strategy needs to tackle these decision-making hurdles head-on. It's not enough to showcase your product's value. You need to break down the decision-making process into manageable steps, providing clarity and reducing the weight of choice. Think of it as offering a guiding hand through the maze of options. By simplifying information, presenting clear comparisons, and addressing decision-making anxieties, you help prospects move from paralysis to action. This accelerates the sales cycle and builds stronger, more confident relationships with your buyers.

What can we do about prospect biases?

Let's look at some common prospect biases and what we can do to address them.

"Have I done enough homework?"

In the digital age, buyers are inundated with information and often question whether they've researched enough. They want to ensure that every decision is well informed and justifiable.

Here's how you can help them overcome this bias:

- **Offer examples of best practices.** Share compelling case studies and success stories that showcase how your solution has delivered outstanding results for others. These real-world examples act as proof points, demonstrating how similar challenges have been addressed successfully. By highlighting best practices, you not only reassure prospects, but also provide them with a benchmark for what success looks like.

- **Offer professional recommendations.** Position yourself as a trusted advisor by providing expert insights and professional guidance. Whether it's through white papers, industry reports, or personalized consultations, your recommendations should reflect a deep understanding of the buyers' needs and the industry landscape. This expert input helps bridge the gap between their research and the practical application of your solution.

- **Steer their research.** Guide prospects through their research process by offering curated content and resources. Create comprehensive guides, checklists, or toolkits highlighting the critical factors they should consider. By curating their research journey, you simplify their decision-making process and ensure they are exposed to the most relevant and impactful information. This proactive approach demonstrates your commitment to their success and positions you as a valuable resource.

Implication: By addressing the "Have I done enough homework?" bias, you reduce the uncertainty and overwhelm that buyers face. Clear examples, expert recommendations, and guided research help them feel more confident in their decisions. It's about making their journey smoother and ensuring they see you as a knowledgeable ally in their decision-making process. This approach builds trust and significantly enhances the likelihood of you closing the deal.

"How do I ensure I get the proposed outcome?"

Once buyers have decided to consider your solution, they naturally wonder about the certainty of achieving the promised results. They're concerned about whether your solution will deliver on its promises and how it will impact their specific situation.

Here's how to address this critical concern:

- **Explain the process.** Lay out a transparent step-by-step process that illustrates how your solution will be implemented and how it will deliver the expected results. Break down each stage—from onboarding to execution—and highlight your actions to ensure success. By providing a transparent overview, you help prospects visualize the journey and understand how you'll support them every step of the way.

- **Tailor the process.** Demonstrate that your approach is not one-size-fits-all. Customize your process to align with the prospect's unique needs and objectives. Show how you'll adapt your solution to their particular context, whether that's by adjusting your strategies, integrating with their existing systems, or accommodating specific requirements. Personalization reassures prospects that you're committed to addressing their challenges and achieving their desired outcomes.

- **Show follow-up and measurement.** Assure prospects that you're not just delivering a solution and walking away. Outline how you'll track and measure the impact of your solution to ensure it's meeting their expectations. Share details about your follow-up procedures, such as regular check-ins, performance reviews, and feedback mechanisms. By emphasizing your commitment to ongoing evaluation and support, you build confidence in your ability to deliver sustained value.

Implication: Addressing the "How do I ensure I get the proposed outcome?" bias requires demonstrating a thorough, customized, and accountable approach. By clearly explaining the process, tailoring it to the prospect's needs, and showing your commitment to follow-up and measurement, you alleviate concerns about the effectiveness of your solution. This approach strengthens their trust in your capabilities and reinforces your role as a dependable partner in their success.

"How do I ensure I don't make the wrong decision?"

When buyers are grappling with FOMU, their anxiety is centered around the potential risks and consequences of their choice. They're worried about investing in a solution that might not deliver as promised or could lead to complications.

Here's how to address these concerns effectively:

- **Establish trust.** Build a solid foundation of trust by setting realistic expectations and developing a genuine rapport with the prospect. Share honest insights about what your solution can achieve and acknowledge any limitations. Being transparent and approachable creates an atmosphere where buyers feel comfortable discussing their concerns and are more likely to trust your guidance. Trust is vital in mitigating fears and moving prospects toward a confident decision.

- **Take risk off the table.** Minimize the perceived risk by offering guarantees, trial periods, or flexible terms that allow prospects to test your solution before fully committing. For instance, you might provide a satisfaction guarantee, a pilot program, or a money-back offer. These risk-reducing measures can reassure buyers that they won't be left high and dry if the solution doesn't meet their expectations, making them more willing to take the plunge.

- **Discuss risk vs. reward.** Help buyers make an informed decision by clearly outlining your solution's potential benefits and risks. Present a balanced view highlighting the rewards of choosing your solution, such as improved efficiency or cost savings, while addressing potential risks. Use data, testimonials, and case studies to support your claims and provide a realistic picture of what prospects can expect. This clarity lets them weigh the risks against the rewards and feel more confident in their decision.

Implication: Addressing the "How do I ensure I don't make the wrong decision?" bias involves building trust, mitigating risks, and providing a precise risk-reward analysis. By establishing a reliable relationship, removing perceived risks, and helping buyers understand the trade-offs, you reduce their anxiety and facilitate a more confident decision-making process. This approach reassures prospects and strengthens their commitment to choosing your solution.

A recurring theme in this chapter has been the building of trust between you and your customers. Trust is essential in moving your customers toward becoming your strategic partners, loyal and committed to you and your solutions.

That is what we will cover in the next chapter.

6
Exploring Partnership

How valuable are you to your customers right now? In the high-stakes world of B2B sales, this is the question you need to confront head-on.

If your customers woke up tomorrow and had to choose between you and another supplier, would it even be a tough decision, or would they search their contacts and find someone cheaper or faster without thinking twice? Are you another vendor in a sea of options, easily replaceable when the next big deal comes, or have you positioned yourself as a strategic partner—an integral part of your customers' business success, someone they can't imagine operating without?

If you haven't reached that coveted status, you're leaving the door open for your competitors to swoop in and claim it. Trust me, they're gunning for that spot. The real question is, are you?

One sale isn't enough

In today's ultra-competitive B2B landscape, just making the sale isn't enough. A proper strategy should go beyond closing deals and build more profound, meaningful relationships that elevate you from a mere vendor to a strategic partner.

That's the Holy Grail of B2B sales: reaching a level where your customer sees you not just as a provider of products or services, but as a trusted advisor essential to their long-term growth and success. However, achieving this status isn't something that simply happens. It's the result of a deliberate, thoughtful approach. It requires you to shift how you think about delivering value, and it means reimagining your role in the eyes of your customers.

Let's break down how you can take your customer relationships to the next level and become the strategic partner they didn't even know they needed.

Gunning for the Holy Grail

The journey from being a replaceable vendor to becoming a strategic partner is a transformation process. It's about moving up a value ladder where, at each step, you deepen your connection and increase the trust your customer places in you.

The question is: where does your organization stand today? Are you at the bottom, vulnerable to being replaced, or are you climbing toward that coveted position of strategic partnership?

Let's break it down into four distinct stages.

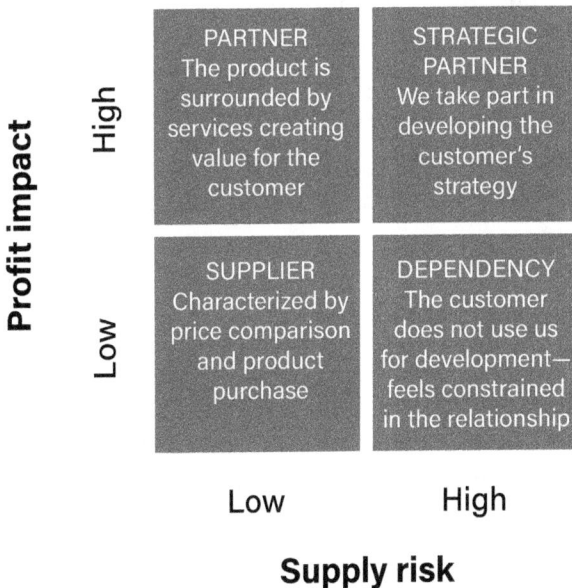

	Low Supply risk	**High** Supply risk
High Profit impact	PARTNER The product is surrounded by services creating value for the customer	STRATEGIC PARTNER We take part in developing the customer's strategy
Low Profit impact	SUPPLIER Characterized by price comparison and product purchase	DEPENDENCY The customer does not use us for development— feels constrained in the relationship

The four stages of partnership (source: Krajlic)

Watch the video: Go to https://salesmarketingmastery.com/video/partnership or scan the QR code for insights and inspiration.

Stage 1: Dependency

At the bottom of the ladder, we have dependency—arguably the most dangerous place to be. In this stage, your customer views your product or service as a means to an end: something they use because they need it, without seeing any more profound value. You're essentially a commodity, and that means your relationship is fragile. The customer feels constrained by the need to work with you, so has no strong loyalty toward you. If someone swoops in with a better price, faster service, or a shinier offer, you're gone. In the customer's mind, you're easily replaceable, just a cog in their machine.

What's the problem?

Your organization isn't adding enough value beyond the basics at this level. If your client portfolio feels more like a series of transactions where your customers are doing you a favor, it's time to rethink your approach.

How can you shift from being just another supplier on their list to a critical player in their strategy? The key lies in looking for ways to become indispensable, showing your customers why they need you and can't afford to lose you.

Stage 2: Supplier

Climbing one rung higher, you reach the level of being a supplier. At this stage, you've moved beyond dependency—customers now recognize the value you bring, but here's the catch: they still see you as one of many. You've become a known entity, but not yet a trusted partner, and that means, despite your efforts, you're still part of a revolving door of options.

In this position, price is the dominant factor in customers' decision making. They evaluate you alongside other suppliers and compare offerings based mainly on cost. Yes, they value your product or service, but their loyalty is shaky. They may enjoy working with you, but what if a competitor offers a better price tomorrow? They'll make the switch. You're not indispensable yet; you're a vendor in their eyes, interchangeable with anyone else who can meet their needs at a lower cost.

What's the problem?

While being a supplier means you're providing something worthwhile, your relationship with your customers is still purely transactional. The challenge here is to escape the constant price war and shift the conversation away from cost alone.

If you can't differentiate yourself, you'll always be at the mercy of someone else's discount or aggressive offer. You need to find a way to stand out and move beyond just being the best price on the market. The goal is to transition from being a supplier to something more meaningful.

How do you do that? It starts by focusing on value beyond price—offering solutions, advice, and expertise that make you more than another option.

Stage 3: Partner

Reaching the level of partner is a significant leap. You've done more than provide a product or service at this stage—you've built trust.

Your customers now recognize that you're offering more than just competitive pricing; they see the value of your expertise, advice, and problem-solving capabilities. The transactional nature of your relationship begins to fade, and it evolves into something more collaborative.

As partners, your customers stop shopping around whenever they need a solution. They come to you because they appreciate your value beyond just the product. You're now solving their problems, offering strategic insights, and helping them achieve their objectives. There's a mutual understanding that you're more than a supplier—you're part of their success story.

However, there's a critical distinction: while they rely on you, you're not yet indispensable. You've earned their trust, but the relationship is still largely tied to your ability to deliver value. If something changes—if you stop providing solutions or a competitor offers something compelling—they might reconsider the partnership.

You're a key player, but not yet irreplaceable.

This phase is about deepening the relationship. To move from partner to strategic partner, you must shift your focus from simply solving problems to actively shaping the customers' strategy. This is where you move from being helpful to critical to their long-term vision. The groundwork has been laid, and now it's time to elevate the relationship.

Stage 4: Strategic partner

At the pinnacle of the value ladder is the role of strategic partner—the coveted Holy Grail in B2B sales. Reaching this level means you've transcended the traditional boundaries of being a vendor or problem solver. You've become a trusted advisor, an integral part of your customer's decision-making process.

When your customer turns to you for solutions and guidance on their long-term strategy, you know you've reached this top tier. As a strategic partner, you're seen as indispensable. Your relationship is no longer transactional; it's deeply intertwined with your success. You've earned a seat at the table when big decisions are made because your input shapes your customer's future.

At this point, price ceases to be a deciding factor. Your customers aren't comparing you to the competition or shopping around—they recognize that your value goes far beyond cost. It's not about the price tag; it's about the growth, innovation, and success that your partnership drives.

The question isn't whether they'll work with you—it's how deeply they'll rely on you. Your organization becomes a key player in their vision for the future, and your success becomes mutual. This level of partnership is where you move from simply meeting needs to actively co-creating value. You're shaping your customers' path forward, helping them navigate challenges and seize opportunities.

This kind of collaboration is rare and is the ultimate position to strive for in B2B sales. For you to reach this level, your strategy must focus on deepening relationships, anticipating needs, and proactively delivering value before your customers even realize they need it. This requires commitment, foresight, and a genuine investment in their success.

Where do you stand on this ladder? More importantly, what steps can you take to move from being just another option to becoming the strategic partner your customers can't live without? The answers to both of those questions lie in examining your paradigms. Let's discuss that next.

The key to climbing the ladder

To ascend the ladder toward becoming a strategic partner, you must understand and adjust the paradigms shaping how your organization delivers value.

How you approach sales and communicate your worth significantly impacts where you stand in your customers' eyes. Let's break down the three primary sales value paradigms and how each determines your position on the value ladder.

Product value

The product alone represents the value

Communication
- Information
- Persuasion
- Convince
- Transaction of products

Focus
- Price
- Content
- Conditions

Solution value

The product is part of a solution in the form of services and products or relationships

Communication
- Identifying and strengthening needs
- Match with a solution

Focus
- Solution
- Customer needs
- Advice

Purpose value

The product is a driver for value, but content and solutions are created in cooperation

Communication
- Dialogue and curiosity
- Proactivity and transparency
- Future focus

Focus
- Value
- Benefits of cooperation
- Third-party value

Sales philosophy paradigms

Product value

In the product value paradigm, the focus is entirely on the product itself.

The selling process here is transactional, revolving around giving potential buyers information about the product's features and price. You're working hard to persuade the buyer that your product is superior to your competitors', with the primary motivator often being the best deal you can offer.

In this paradigm, you communicate facts—specs, functionality, cost savings—but your relationship with the customer is strictly business. It's all about making the sale. There's little to no focus on the customer's specific needs or long-term goals, and your involvement ends when the deal is closed.

While this approach can certainly lead to sales, it's a dead-end in terms of fostering a deeper, more valuable relationship. You're simply a vendor—one of many—and easily replaceable.

Price comparisons will dominate the conversation, and loyalty will be thin. Your customer views you as someone to meet their immediate needs, but not someone to help them grow or solve more significant challenges.

If your business resonates with the product value paradigm, you must shift your focus from selling a product to solving a problem. Only then can you start climbing the ladder toward partnership.

Solution value

In the solution value paradigm, the focus shifts from simply selling a product to building a relationship with the customer. It's no longer about pushing a specific offering; it's about understanding your customer's unique challenges and tailoring your solutions to meet their needs.

In this paradigm, the communication style transforms from transactional to consultative. You're not just presenting features and benefits; you're diving deep into their business, diagnosing problems, and recommending solutions that directly address them. The key here is that you're not trying to sell them something they don't need; instead, you're positioning yourself as a trusted advisor who can solve real problems.

This shift in mindset begins to move you up the value ladder. You're no longer just a vendor, but are starting to be seen as a partner. Your customers appreciate your input, and you're now in a position where they trust your judgment and rely on your expertise. They value your insight beyond the products you offer.

However, while you've earned their trust, you're not yet at the top. There's still room to grow. You're solving your customers' problems, but haven't fully embedded yourself into their strategy. In the solution value paradigm, your relationship is still centered around specific needs and solutions rather than long-term goals and vision. The challenge is evolving from a problem solver into a strategic partner.

Purpose value

The most effective paradigm in B2B sales is purpose value. In this paradigm, you and your customer work toward a shared vision. Your relationship transcends traditional boundaries. It's no longer about pushing products or solving immediate problems, but co-creating solutions that align with your customer's long-term goals.

In the purpose value paradigm, you've bought into your customer's objectives and become a crucial ally in helping them achieve those goals. Your communication is no longer just responsive; it's proactive. You anticipate their needs before they even express them. You're transparent, sharing insights and resources openly, and both sides are fully invested in each other's success.

This type of relationship transforms everything. You're not simply a supplier or a partner anymore—you're part of your customer's strategic future. Every interaction is framed by a shared commitment to achieving a broader vision, not just fulfilling short-term needs. You're thinking ahead rather than reacting to the present, and this future-focused approach makes the relationship deeply collaborative.

Now you're not just providing value, but sharing in the customer's long-term success. This is the essence of a strategic partnership—where you and your customer are linked by transactions or problem-solving and a mutual drive toward achieving great things together.

This paradigm is the ultimate goal of B2B sales, where you've ascended the ladder and helped build success alongside your customer.

Implication: Where your organization sits on the value ladder determines how indispensable you are to your customers. Moving from a product-focused approach to a purpose-driven partnership, you climb the ladder toward strategic partnership—the Holy Grail of B2B sales.

Ask yourself: "What paradigm are we operating in, and how can we evolve our approach to provide more profound, meaningful value?"

Aligning your sales philosophy

When it comes to sales, your company's philosophy and approach make all the difference in how you're perceived by customers. It's not just about the product you're selling—it's about how you're selling it.

Where does your company stand on this sales philosophy continuum?

Transaction selling	SPIN selling	Value-based selling	Challenger sales	Co-creation
The customer must be convinced	We help the customer to make the choice and understand their needs	Our solutions are the best—we guide you to solutions	We bring unique knowledge and insights	We are on the same side as the customer

The further you move along this path, the more likely you are to be seen as a strategic partner—the most valued and sought-after position in B2B sales.

Watch the video: Go to https://salesmarketingmastery.com/video/sales-philosophy or scan the QR code.

Convince the customer

This is the most basic level of sales philosophy. Here, the focus is on convincing the customer why your product is superior. It's a traditional features-and-benefits-driven approach where the goal is to highlight what makes your product better than the competition. While this can work, it leads to transactional relationships where price is often the crucial factor, not relationships.

Assist the customer in choosing

When you move along the sales philosophy continuum, the focus shifts from pure persuasion to helping the customer understand why your solution is the best fit for their needs. It's not just about listing features; it's about guiding the customer through their options and making the decision process easier for them. At this stage, your team starts to act more like consultants rather than salespeople.

Enable the customer with solutions

Here, the relationship deepens as you position your product as a tool that enables the customer to achieve their goals. The focus is on solving the customer's problems and adding tangible value. Your sales approach becomes centered on understanding their challenges and offering tailored solutions, which builds trust and rapport.

Bring unique insights and knowledge

At this level, you go beyond providing solutions— you bring unique insights that help the customer see their problems in a new light. You're not just solving existing issues; you're enabling them to identify new opportunities for growth and improvement.

This approach positions you as a thought leader and trusted advisor, someone who adds value beyond the product itself.

Be part of the customer's team on a shared mission

This is the pinnacle of the sales philosophy continuum. Here, you and the customer are on the same side, working together as part of a shared mission. You've moved beyond the role of vendor or even advisor; you're a true strategic partner. The customer sees you as integral to their long-term success, and price becomes a secondary concern because of the deep value and trust you've built.

Why alignment matters

The further your company moves along this continuum, the better positioned you are to become a strategic partner—the ultimate spot in B2B selling. When your sales philosophy aligns with a collaborative, customer-first approach, you build stronger relationships and create more value for your clients. This not only leads to higher customer retention and loyalty, but also positions you as a key part of the customer's strategy, making your solution indispensable.

Before we shift the focus onto the customers you are targeting and whether they're the right fit for your business, you need to make sure that you give your organization the best chance of cultivating a strategic partnership with your ideal client. It all starts with asking yourself: "Where is my company now on the alignment continuum? How does that dictate the next steps we must take?"

7

Who Are You Targeting?

How confident are you that you're targeting the right people in your B2B sales efforts? Are you putting your time and energy into prospects that can catapult your business forward, or are you wasting resources on leads that will never get you where you need to go?

In the high-stakes world of B2B sales, it doesn't matter how slick your pitch is, how hard you work, or how innovative your product is—if you're chasing the wrong prospects, you won't hit your sales targets. You could have the most charismatic sales team and the best product in the market, but if you're not engaging with the right audience, you're setting yourself up to fail.

How do you ensure you're aiming at the right target? Successful selling isn't just about effort—it's about strategy. You can grind all day, but all that work won't move the needle if you're talking to the wrong people.

In reality, many organizations waste time chasing leads that will never convert. Thought leader in the field of influence Robert Cialdini (2006) notes that tailored communication based on specific buyer needs significantly enhances persuasion and engagement. Smart selling starts with knowing exactly who your ideal prospects are and focusing your efforts on those most likely to deliver value.

In this chapter, we'll unpack the steps to identify, assess, and segment your ideal customers, ensuring every effort is directed toward prospects that can drive actual results. At the end of the day, it's not about chasing every lead—it's about targeting the right ones.

Establishing your customer platform

Are you basing your sales efforts on your customers' purchases or considering their full potential? How often have you categorized a customer based on what they've spent, only to miss out on what they could bring?

Many businesses fall into the trap of pigeonholing customers based on their past behavior. They'll look at a customer's purchase and use that to gauge future potential, but this approach is flawed because it ignores the bigger picture—what your customer could achieve with you if you unlocked their full potential.

Just because a customer has spent $10,000 doesn't mean they can't pay $50,000 or more. The challenge is knowing who has that potential and how to engage them in a way that maximizes it.

To put this into context, take a look at the graph below:

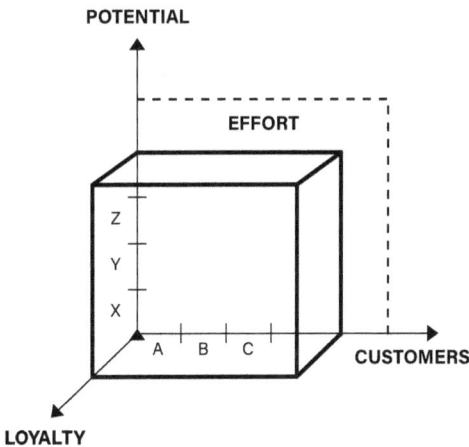

Customer platform

Regarding potential, customer C is worth much more than customers B and A. Therefore, investing more effort into C makes sense, which results in even more loyalty and a more substantial customer base for a B2B organization.

Go through your customer and client list and plot something similar. You'll get insights into how you should be devoting your organization's most valuable resources and effort.

Watch the video: Go to https://salesmarketingmastery.com/video/mastering or scan the QR code for insights and inspiration.

Establish your segmentation criteria

Are you wasting time on leads that will never convert while your ideal customers slip through the cracks? How often are you chasing prospects who won't deliver while the most promising opportunities sit untapped?

Effective selling isn't just about finding leads, but finding suitable leads. That means intelligent segmentation. When you treat every prospect the same, you dilute your efforts. Time is wasted chasing dead-end leads, while high-potential customers—those who could impact your bottom line—don't get the attention they deserve. Segmentation allows you to tailor your approach and focus your energy where it counts. It's not enough to consider superficial factors like industry or location. To truly segment effectively, you must dig deeper and categorize prospects based on three critical dimensions: profile, behavior, and need. Let's look at each.

Need

The importance of the product for the buyer
Price, technology, or service
Buying impact and degree of centralisation
Understanding the context
Buying infrastructure

Behavior

Sales and growth focus
Influenced by sales efforts
Loyal
Open to innovation

Profile

Business
Geography
Number of employess

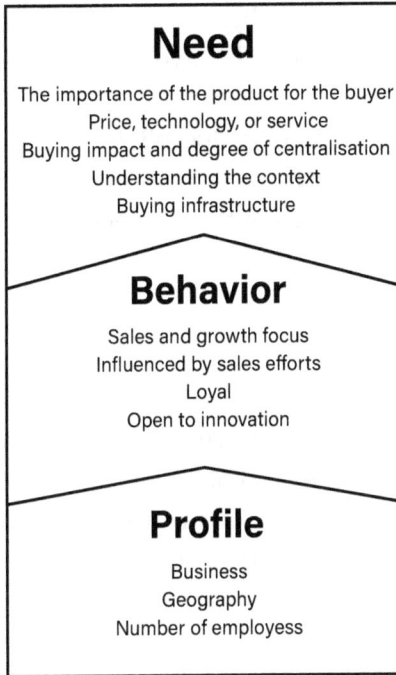

Segmentation criteria

Watch the video: Go to https://salesmarketingmastery.com/video/segmentation or scan the QR code for insights and inspiration.

Profile

This is the basic demographic data. What kind of business is your prospect in? Where are they located geographically? How big is their operation, and how many employees do they have?

While this information doesn't tell you everything, it's a starting point to help you group your prospects and understand their surface-level characteristics.

Behavior

This level digs deeper into how the customer operates. Are they focused on growth, or are they stagnant? Do they have a track record of loyalty with their vendors, or do they jump ship for the next shiny offer? How open are they to adopting new products, services, or innovations? Just as important, what's your current relationship with them?

These behavioral indicators can give you insight into customers' potential and help you determine how best to engage them.

Need

At this stage, you're getting to the heart of the matter. How vital is your product or service to the customer's overall strategy? What impact can your offering have on their long-term goals and business objectives? If your product or service can make or break their success, they're worth prioritizing. The more you understand their needs, the better positioned you are to offer value that resonates.

By segmenting your customers through this three-tiered approach, you'll be able to better qualify prospects, zeroing in on those who align with your business goals. The result? You'll stop chasing leads that never convert and focus on building relationships with the ones that matter most.

Fit to sales approach

Even when you have a meticulously segmented list of prospects, sales success hinges on one critical factor: alignment. Not every prospect will be a natural fit for your sales strategy, and that's OK. What isn't OK is trying to push a sale with a one-size-fits-all approach. It's like using a hammer when you really need a wrench—you'll waste time and energy, and it won't work in the end.

Recognizing fit is about understanding whether your sales methodology, communication style, and value proposition align with a prospect's needs, decision-making process, and goals. The better the fit, the smoother and more successful your sales efforts will be. That raises an important question: how does one evaluate fit? Here are some questions that can help provide answers.

Does your approach match the customer's buying process?

Every company has its own way of making purchasing decisions. Some are fast-paced, while others take a more systematic approach. Your job is to determine how your prospects like to buy and whether your sales approach is in sync.

If your sales strategy is consultative, but your prospect wants a straightforward no-frills transaction, the mismatch will hinder progress.

How well do they align with your sales style?

Think about how you position your product or service. Are you focused on long-term solutions or do you sell quick wins? Do you emphasize personal relationships or data-driven results?

Some prospects will respond well to your natural sales style, while others won't. The key is to identify those whose values and expectations align with how you sell. If there's a fit, it'll feel seamless.

Can you deliver the right value at the right time?

Timing matters. A prospect might need what you're offering, but if they aren't ready to buy or your sales cycle doesn't match theirs, it can lead to frustration. Understanding when and how your solution fits into their broader plans ensures you're offering value when they're ready to act.

You can focus your efforts on the most promising opportunities by evaluating your prospects through the lens of how well they fit your sales approach. You'll stop trying to convert leads that were never the right fit and instead spend your time and energy on prospects naturally aligned with your strategy.

A useful way of representing the quality of your clients in this context is through a graph such as the one you see below.

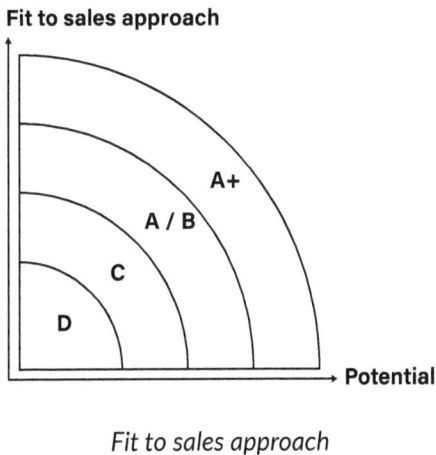

Fit to sales approach

The ones labeled A+ are your best clients in terms of potential, so you prioritize your best resources to target and serve them.

AN EXERCISE

As we conclude this book's first part, I'd like to engage you in a little exercise. It's something I tend to ask any new client to do if they're having problems with how well their company is performing in terms of sales.

I ask them to consider what factors they believe are causing their misery. Then, they fill out the table below.

Watch the video: Go to https://salesmarketingmastery.com/files/sales-trend-analysis or scan the QR code, or simply copy out the table to fill in for your organization.

Let me provide you with a short guide on how to fill out the table.

External factors:

- **Market.** How would you describe the general outlook of the market you are involved in?
- **Customer behavior.** How are people buying? What are they buying?
- **Value proposition.** What kinds of value propositions are people responding to?

Market

Customer behavior

Value proposition

Sales management (targets and rewards)

Knowledge and competencies

Sales process

Sales organization

Internal factors:

- **Sales management.** How well do you actively organize your team to ensure it accomplishes its objective?

- **Knowledge and competencies.** How knowledgeable is your team about your product/service and sales closing tactics?

- **Sales process.** What does your sales process look like? What happens before you close a deal with a prospect?

- **Sales organization.** How have you organized your sales team in terms of hierarchy and who answers to who?

When people take on this exercise, I usually get a keen insight into their thoughts and how I should help them. I find that most clients who are out of scope with the market (or soon will be) fill out most of the stuff on the left side and very little on the right side. That's often a sign of disaster.

Remember what I said before? External factors are outside your control. Internal factors (the right side) are what you can do something about. Instead of complaining about what's out there, how about you adapt your internal matters to align with the changing environment? Make sense? Cool.

I'll see you in the next part.

PART TWO
STRUCTURE AND PROCESS

N ow that we've laid the groundwork with strategy, it's time to shift our focus to something just as important—structure and process. If strategy is the what and why of your B2B sales efforts, then structure and process are the how. It's not enough to know your goals or have a solid plan for targeting the right prospects. You need a well-defined, repeatable system to turn that strategy into measurable results. This is where so many organizations fall short. They might have a great vision, but without a strong structure to support it and a process to execute it, even the best strategy will struggle to get off the ground.

Think of it like building a house. The strategy is your blueprint—the grand design—but without a sturdy framework (structure) and a step-by-step construction plan (process), you'll end up with a pile of materials and no house to show for it.

In this part of the book, we'll explore how to build that sturdy framework and develop a seamless process that will allow your strategy to shine. I'll break down the key components of structure and process, and show you how to create a cohesive system that aligns your team, optimizes your resources, and consistently delivers results.

Let's dive in and start turning your strategy into action.

8
Achieving Sales Efficiency

How many sales are slipping through the cracks because your process isn't operating like a well-oiled machine? What would it mean for your bottom line if every step in your sales pipeline was optimized for maximum efficiency?

Imagine setting a bold sales goal—$10 million, perhaps—and being absolutely confident in your ability to achieve it. No guesswork, no winging it. Just a clear, actionable path. How do you make that kind of precision a reality?

Every executive dreams of having an efficient, perfectly synchronized sales team that hits ambitious targets, which become not just a possibility, but a near certainty. A team that doesn't merely chase leads, but turns them into paying customers with predictable success.

Here's the question that haunts even the most seasoned leaders: how do you make this happen? What's the formula for turning a good sales team into a high-performance engine that reliably hits its goals? Instinctively, many believe that the answer lies in the early stages of the sales process—generating more leads, making more calls, and sending more emails. After all, more effort should equal more results, right?

Wrong.

Here's the catch: efficiency doesn't come from just ramping up your efforts at the start. It's about mastering the end game. The real magic happens when you work backward from your ultimate goal, breaking down every step and calculating what it takes to hit your target.

In this chapter, I will show you how to unlock the power of this backward approach—how to reverse-engineer your sales success by understanding the entire process from close to the start. When you master that, you don't just achieve efficiency—you achieve predictable, scalable success.

Understanding the sales ladder

Think of the sales process as being like climbing a ladder. Each rung represents a critical step in your journey toward closing a deal, and just like with a real ladder, you can't skip a rung and expect to reach the top without stumbling.

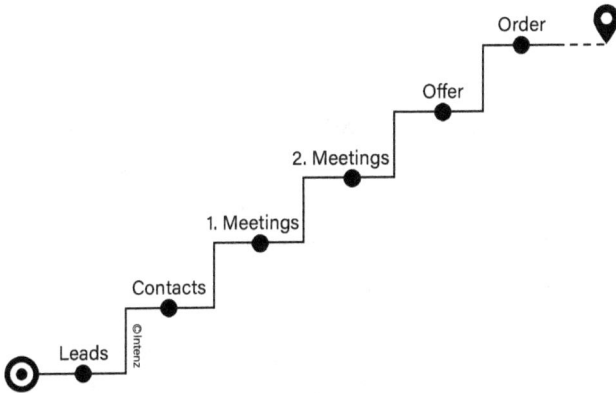

Way to order

Watch the video: Go to https://salesmarketingmastery.com/video/way-to-orders or scan the QR code for insights and inspiration.

The goal of achieving sales efficiency lies in understanding this ladder intimately and ensuring that each step is executed precisely. The truth is that success at one step is necessary to make the next one possible. If you falter on any step, you risk derailing the entire process.

What are these key steps? Let's break it down:

- **Checking the lead list.** begins with having the right leads to work with. This step ensures your lead pool is well researched and aligned with your ideal customer profile.

- **Qualifying leads and developing contacts.** Next comes the critical process of separating the wheat from the chaff. This is where you identify which leads are worth pursuing and start nurturing those early relationships.

- **Securing the first meeting.** Here's where things start to get real. Securing that first meeting should feel like a natural next step if you've done your job qualifying leads. It's where your initial contact turns into an actual conversation.

- **Securing the second meeting.** The second meeting is a key milestone where you start building momentum and laying the foundation for an offer. It's where the lead evolves into a real prospect.

- **Making the offer.** You've laid the groundwork and earned trust, and now it's time to make your pitch. This is where you present your solution, tailored to the prospect's needs, and aim to convert them into a client.

- **Closing the deal (scoring the client).** Finally, the last step on the ladder—the ultimate goal. You're here to win the deal, seal the relationship, and transform that prospect into a paying customer.

Each step on the ladder builds on the one before it. Miss a step, and everything that follows could crumble. It's not just about climbing as fast as possible— it's about ensuring each step is secure before moving forward. The more smoothly you transition between steps, the more efficient and effective your sales process becomes.

Understanding this ladder is the first step in mastering sales efficiency. Once you know what each rung looks like, you can start figuring out exactly what it takes to move up the ladder—and that's where the real magic happens.

Reverse-engineering sales goals

Here's where most people get it wrong—they think sales efficiency is all about generating more leads. The real secret is about starting with the end in mind. Instead of beginning with lead generation, you work backward from your ultimate sales goal. Why? When you reverse-engineer the process, you gain absolute clarity on achieving your targets. If you want to hit that ambitious $10 million sales target, don't just focus on the number of leads you need. Start with your final goal—closing deals—and trace your steps backward.

AN EXAMPLE: The power of reverse engineering

Let's say you've set a target of $10 million in sales. You know that your average order size is $10,000, so simple math tells you that you'll need to close 1,000 clients ($10 million divided by $10,000) to reach your goal.

How do you get there? This is where the sales ladder comes in.

To close one client, let's say the data from your past sales cycles shows you need:

- One offer to convert the client
- Three second meetings to lead to one offer
- Three first meetings to get to one second meeting
- Six calls to qualified leads to land one first meeting

That's 54 leads for every sale ($1 \times 3 \times 3 \times 6 = 54$).

Now multiply that by your target number of clients. To close 1,000 clients, you will need 54,000 leads (54 leads per client × 1,000 clients = 54,000 leads).

Here's the beauty of working backward—when you break it down into these concrete numbers, sales efficiency becomes a predictable science, not a guessing game. You know precisely how many leads you need, how many meetings you need to schedule, and how many offers you need to make to reach your goal. By reverse-engineering your sales target, you're no longer flying blind. You have a roadmap that connects every stage of the process, and every move you make is intentional.

At its core, sales efficiency is about understanding the numbers at each process stage and using those numbers to forecast success. The result? A finely tuned, high-performing sales team equipped to deliver on ambitious targets—because they know exactly what it takes to get there.

Breaking down each step for maximum efficiency

Lead list

If you're filling your pipeline with weak leads, you only set yourself up for disappointment. The efficiency of your sales process starts with the lead list. It's not about sheer volume—it's about targeting the right people. How can you improve your lead list to make each step of the sales ladder more efficient? First, refine your criteria for what qualifies as a strong lead. Are they representing the right size organization? Do they have the budget? Are they in the right industry?

By focusing on leads with high potential, you can ensure that every call and meeting you make is with someone worth your time.

Qualifying leads

This is where efficiency begins to take shape. It is where you determine whether a prospect is worth pursuing, but it's more than just ticking boxes. Is the prospect open to new ideas? Do they have decision-making power? Do they need what you're offering?

Effective lead qualification is the first safeguard against wasted effort. The more precisely you can qualify your leads, the fewer dead-ends you'll hit. Use criteria like urgency, budget, and decision-making power to qualify leads who are more likely to move through your sales funnel.

First and second meetings

You've got the meeting—now what?

The first and second meetings are pivotal because they either set the stage for an offer or end the conversation early. The key to optimizing these meetings is preparation. Know your prospect's pain points, anticipate their objections, and tailor your pitch accordingly. Don't overwhelm them with everything you've got—focus on what's most relevant to them. By delivering a pitch that addresses their immediate needs and shows a clear path to success, you'll significantly increase the likelihood of moving them to the next step.

Making the offer

Many salespeople stumble here because they don't tailor the offer to the client's needs. You've presented a solid pitch, but it won't stand out if your offer feels generic. Personalization is your secret weapon here. Craft an offer that feels like it was made specifically for the client, touching on their pain points, goals, and budget. The more relevant your offer, the harder it will be for them to say no.

Remember, an irresistible offer isn't just about price—it's about perceived value.

Scoring the client

Closing the deal doesn't happen in a vacuum. It's the result of everything you've done leading up to that point, but don't let up when you're near the finish line—this is where you need to be sharp.

Use tactics like limited-time offers or exclusive deals to create urgency, and always be ready to handle objections with confidence. It's not just about the final offer—it's about reinforcing the value you've demonstrated throughout the process. When it's done right, scoring the client is a natural conclusion to a series of well-executed steps.

The role of metrics in achieving efficiency

You can't improve what you don't measure. To achieve actual sales efficiency, you need to track the right metrics at each stage of the sales ladder. These key performance indicators (KPIs) offer insights into how well your team is performing and where adjustments are needed.

Here are some of the most critical metrics to track:

- **Lead qualification rate:** How many leads make it past the qualification stage? This tells you whether your lead list and qualification process are strong or if you're wasting time on weak prospects.

- **Meeting conversion rate:** How many first meetings turn into second meetings? This indicates how compelling your initial pitch is and whether it's resonating with potential clients.

- **Offer conversion rate:** How many offers lead to deals? This measures the effectiveness of your proposals and whether you're tailoring them well enough to close the sale.

- **Close rate:** How many qualified leads turn into paying clients? This is the ultimate measure of success and reflects the overall efficiency of your sales process.

By focusing on these KPIs, you can pinpoint the bottle-necks in your sales process and address them directly.

Tracking and adjusting

It's not enough to track these metrics—you must act on them. Regularly monitoring your KPIs allows you to spot inefficiencies early. For example, if you notice that your meeting-to-offer conversion rate is low, it could mean that your initial pitch needs work. Suppose your close rate is lower than expected. In that case, your offers may not be as compelling as they should be, or you're missing out on personalization.

The goal here is continuous improvement. Use the data to make informed adjustments. For instance:

- **Tweak your messaging:** If meetings aren't converting, revise your pitch to better align with the prospect's pain points.

- **Improve offer customization:** If your offer-to-close rate is lacking, focus on refining how you present your offer to make it feel more tailored.

- **Revisit lead qualification:** If too few deals are closing, ensure you're targeting the right prospects from the start.

AN EXAMPLE: Turning projections into results

Remember being the company CEO in the previous example who set a lofty sales goal—$10 million in new business for the year? You've broken down your sales process and determined that, on average, each deal is worth $10,000. To reach the 1,000 closed deals you require, you've realized you'll need to work with 54,000 leads. This knowledge empowers you to scale your lead-generation efforts to meet the goal.

However, there's more: you need to track each process stage throughout the year. Then you can quickly adjust your strategy if you're falling short in one area.

Say you're not securing enough second meetings. Maybe you can refine your pitch or improve your lead qualification process.

You stay on course to hit your sales target by consistently monitoring your metrics and adjusting your processes wherever there's a bottleneck.

The real power of metrics lies in their ability to inform actionable changes. By tracking the correct numbers and adjusting your tactics accordingly, you can systematically improve the efficiency of your sales process.

Forecasting and planning for success

Once you've broken down your sales ladder and identified the key metrics at each step, forecasting becomes less of a guessing game and more of a calculated strategy. You can confidently project your future sales outcomes with a solid grasp of your numbers.

Think of it as creating a roadmap to success. When you know how many leads, meetings, and offers are needed to close deals, you can accurately predict whether or not you'll hit your sales targets.

The beauty of this approach lies in its precision. By understanding the conversion rates at each stage of your process, you can forecast with much greater confidence. For instance, if you know that every 100 leads result in one sale, you can reverse-engineer your entire strategy. Want to close 100 sales? You now know you'll need 10,000 leads.

Efficiency equals predictability

Sales efficiency isn't just about working faster—it's about working smarter. When you have a firm grasp on your numbers, you gain the power of predictability. You no longer have to cross your fingers and hope to hit your sales goals. Instead, you can confidently plan your strategy, forecast success, and make data-driven adjustments. By the time you've mapped out your sales ladder, optimized each step, and locked down your key metrics, you're not just managing a sales team—you're managing a well-oiled machine designed to hit every target you set.

9
Optimizing The Sales Process

Is your sales process working for you or against you? Are you running a finely tuned machine where every part of the process clicks, or are you simply hoping for the best, crossing your fingers every time a prospect enters the funnel?

What if you could transform your sales process into an efficiency engine that doesn't just deliver results, it practically guarantees them? How much more confident would your team feel if they knew, step by step, precisely what needed to be done to close more deals?

Imagine optimizing that process to be even more predictable—tweaking every action, refining every interaction, until your sales engine hums along so smoothly that hitting targets is no longer a hope, but an expectation. What would that mean for your bottom line?

Every sales and marketing team has this same dream, but here's the real challenge. Developing such a process is one thing. Optimizing it to run like clockwork, delivering maximum results at every stage, is another. The first step toward achieving this is often overlooked...

Understanding the customer journey

At the heart of every successful sales process is one simple truth: no sale happens in isolation. Every customer goes on a journey—a predictable path that moves them from recognizing a need to making a final decision.

Understanding this journey is the key to building a sales process that resonates with your prospects and maximizes your chances of closing the deal. If you can meet your customer at each step of their journey, guiding them seamlessly from one stage to the next, your chances of success multiply exponentially.

Your sales process isn't just about your company's goals; it's about aligning those goals with the natural progression of your customer's decision-making process. When you know where your customers are mentally and emotionally at each step, you can tailor your approach to meet them there, offering the proper support, information, and reassurance they need to take the next step. This is the way the customer journey becomes the foundation for every great sales process.

Customer journey				
	Trigger	Consideration	Evaluation	Decision

Sales process				
	Contact	Identify	Solution	Negotiation and acceptance

The sales process and the customer journey

Let's look at the key stages of the customer journey.

1. Search

The journey begins when the customer becomes aware of a need. This could be triggered by a problem they want to solve, an inefficiency they're noticing, or an opportunity they want to seize.

At this stage, they are actively searching for solutions. They may not know the exact solution they need yet, but they know they have an issue that needs fixing. Your goal here is to make sure your solution is discoverable, whether through content marketing, ads, or referrals.

Your sales process response: Position your product or service as the solution. Be present where your customers are searching—whether on Google, social media, or industry forums—and provide educational content highlighting the need you solve.

2. Consider

Once the customer better understands their problem, they start considering different solutions. They're forming a shortlist of potential providers or products at this stage. They're not quite ready to decide, but they're narrowing their options. Your job is to make sure you're on that shortlist.

Your sales process response: Build credibility. Offer case studies, testimonials, and comparisons highlighting why your solution should be a top contender. Focus on showing how your product or service uniquely solves the customer's problem better than others.

3. Evaluate and compare

Now the prospect is digging deeper. They compare their options, weigh the pros and cons, and determine which provider offers the best value for their needs.

They'll pay attention to features, pricing, support, and customer reviews.

Your sales process response: This is where personalization and differentiation matter. Engage your prospect with personalized demos or consultations, tailored messaging, and in-depth comparisons that show why your solution is the perfect fit. Address any lingering doubts or questions head-on.

4. Decide

Finally, after a thorough evaluation, the prospect makes their decision. At this stage, they'll decide based on a combination of factors—perceived value, trust in your brand, fit with their specific needs, and pricing. If you've successfully guided them through the earlier stages, you're now in the best position to close the deal.

Your sales process response: Ensure the customer's decision-making process is as smooth as possible. Provide a clear, straightforward path to closing—whether through a compelling final offer, strong pricing incentives, or simplified contract negotiations. Make the decision to choose your product a no-brainer.

The more closely your sales process aligns with these stages, the more you can influence your prospects' decisions at each step. When your process becomes a natural extension of the customer's journey, you won't just be selling—you'll be guiding prospects toward the best decision for them, which also happens to be you.

Mapping the customer journey to your sales process

To optimize your sales process, it's essential to understand how the customer journey aligns with each step of that process. Why?

Success comes when you engage with your prospects at the right moments—offering guidance and solutions tailored to their needs at each phase of their decision-making journey. By mapping the customer's actions and thoughts to specific stages in your sales process, you ensure your team is doing the right things at the right times, effectively moving the prospect from curiosity to commitment.

Think of it like a relay race. Each handoff—each moment of contact—should be smooth and intentional. If you drop the baton at any stage, you risk losing the prospect's trust or interest.

Mapping their journey into your sales process ensures you never miss a beat, maintaining momentum to the finish line.

	Contact	Need	Solution	Acceptance
	Trigger	Consideration	Evaluation	Decision
Our goal with sales phase				
Our actions— what we do				
Channels / methods				
How to	10%	25%	50%	75%

Let's map the four key stages of the customer journey (search, consider, evaluate and compare, decide) onto a practical four-step sales process. Then you can guide prospects precisely and optimize every interaction's impact.

1. Contact—Customer journey stage: Search

At this stage, the customer is aware of a problem and searching for solutions. Your goal here is simple: make contact. Whether prospects find you through your content, ads, referrals, or inbound inquiries, this is the moment to build awareness and open the lines of communication. It's not about hard selling—it's about making a connection.

Your sales process response: Engage with prospects naturally and helpfully. Use your outreach to offer educational content, insights, or tools to help the prospect better understand their problem. It's about being a guide, not a pushy salesperson. Focus on building rapport, sharing value, and positioning yourself as a trusted resource early on.

2. Need—Customer journey stage: Consider

Now the prospect is starting to narrow down their options. They're comparing providers and thinking more deeply about their specific needs. This is where you need to dive deeper into their pain points. It's not enough to tell them you have a solution—you need to help them articulate their problem and understand how your product or service can specifically solve it.

Your sales process response: Ask insightful questions that dig into the heart of their challenges. Show empathy for their situation and use tailored messaging that speaks to their unique context. The more you can personalize your conversations at this stage, the better your chances of standing out. This is the time to engage in needs analysis, offering consultative insights that position you as an expert who understands the prospect's pain.

3. Solution—Customer journey stage: Evaluate and compare

Here's where the rubber meets the road. Your prospect is now comparing you to your competitors, weighing options, and deciding which solution aligns best with their needs. This is the stage where your offer has to shine. It's not just about features—it's about the total value you bring, including benefits, differentiation, and alignment with the prospect's goals.

Your sales process response: Present your solution as the ideal fit, focusing on how it addresses their needs better than your competitors'. Use case studies, testimonials, and real-world examples to showcase your results.

Personalization remains critical here—tailor your presentations and proposals to reflect the prospect's specific context, concerns, and objectives. This stage is about demonstrating your unique value and making it hard for the prospect to choose anyone else.

4. Negotiate and accept—Customer journey stage: Decide

The final stage is where your prospect is ready to make a decision. However, there may still be a few last-minute hurdles—pricing, contract terms, or internal approvals.

This is where negotiation happens, and your job is to make it as easy as possible for the prospect to say yes. You want to remove any lingering friction and create a win-win situation.

Your sales process response: Be flexible but firm. Address any final objections they might have—whether it's about pricing, terms, or support—and offer solutions that make them feel confident moving forward. At this point, it's less about selling and more about reassuring. Ensure you're clear on the next steps and provide a smooth path to closing. Whether by simplifying contracts, offering a special incentive, or ensuring a seamless onboarding process, you want to make your prospect's decision as easy and risk-free as possible.

By mapping the customer journey to your sales process, you ensure that every interaction is purposeful, personalized, and aligned with the customer's current mindset. This leads to a smoother, more efficient process and increases your chances of success at every stage.

Optimizing each stage of the sales process

To achieve maximum efficiency in your sales process, it's not enough to follow the steps—you need to constantly refine and optimize each stage.

Think of your sales process like a finely tuned machine. Every gear (or step) has to work in perfect harmony to drive momentum and results. If one part is inefficient, the whole system slows down. By optimizing each stage of your sales process, you ensure that every action your team takes is driving you closer to a closed deal, with fewer roadblocks and more wins along the way.

Let's take a detailed look at how you can optimize each step for better outcomes.

1. Contact

This is where you make your initial outreach—whether through cold calling, inbound marketing, email campaigns, or other methods. It's your first interaction with the prospect, and first impressions count. Are you contacting the right people? Are you leveraging the most effective channels?

How to optimize

Lead generation is the foundation of your sales process. If you're casting too wide a net, you'll waste time chasing leads that never convert. If your outreach isn't personalized, you'll fail to capture attention. The key to optimizing this stage is focusing on high-quality leads and using targeted, personalized outreach.

OPTIMIZATION TIP

Leverage data and research to zero in on the most promising leads.

Use tools like customer relationship management (CRM) systems, social media, and analytics to identify the leads with the highest potential to convert. Personalize your outreach—through tailored emails or custom content—to resonate with each prospect's unique needs. Focus on quality over quantity, ensuring that your first contact sets the stage for a successful relationship.

2. Need

At this stage, you're diving deeper into the prospect's situation, uncovering their pain points and understanding their challenges. This is your chance to build trust and position yourself as the expert who can solve their problems.

How to optimize

The key to success here is effective qualification. You must go beyond surface-level needs and dig into the real issues driving the prospect to seek a solution. By understanding their challenges deeper, you can tailor your approach to position your product or service as the ideal fit.

OPTIMIZATION TIP

Ask probing, insightful questions that uncover the actual pain points the prospect is dealing with.

Don't be afraid to go beyond the obvious—dig into how these challenges affect their business, team, or bottom line. The more you understand their problem, the more you can customize your solution to their needs.

Remember: at this stage, you're not just selling a product—you're offering solutions to the prospect's biggest problems. Make sure they see you as the one who "gets" them.

3. Solution

It's time to present your product or service as the best solution to the prospect's problems. Your proposal has to resonate with the prospect's needs, and you need to prove that you're the right choice.

How to optimize

It's all about personalization and proof. A generic pitch won't cut it. The solution you present should feel tailor-made for the prospect's unique situation, and you need to back it up with evidence that it works.

OPTIMIZATION TIP

Use case studies, testimonials, and return on investment (ROI) analysis to prove your solution best fits.

Show examples of how you've solved similar problems for other clients, highlighting the measurable results you've delivered. This isn't just about features—it's about proving the value and impact of your solution. Ensure your presentation or proposal is highly personalized, addressing the prospect's specific pain points and goals. You're not merely selling a product; you're selling success.

4. Negotiate and accept

The prospect is ready to decide, but some objections or concerns may still stand in the way. This is your chance to overcome those last hurdles and guide them toward a yes.

How to optimize

At this stage, closing the deal is less about hard selling and more about removing friction. It would be best to address any remaining objections, offer flexible terms where needed, and make the prospect feel confident they're making the right choice.

OPTIMIZATION TIP

Be prepared to offer a range of flexible terms that make it easy for the prospect to say yes.

Whether by adjusting pricing, offering additional support, or customizing terms, you aim to remove any final objections and make the decision a no-brainer. Focus on the sale's emotional and logical aspects— reassure the customer they're making a smart, strategic choice and that your solution will deliver the desired results. Make the signing process seamless and stress-free, eliminating any barriers that could delay or derail the close.

Optimizing each stage of the sales process means fine-tuning your approach so that every interaction, touchpoint, and conversation drives the sale forward. By continually refining how you engage with prospects at each step, you increase efficiency, reduce wasted effort, and improve your overall success rate. The smoother your sales process, the more predictable your results become.

Tracking the right metrics

You can't optimize what you don't measure. If you're serious about improving your sales process, data has to become your best friend. Business analytics experts Thomas Davenport and Jeanne Harris (2017) argue that data-driven insights lead to more effective decision making and sales process optimization.

Imagine driving a car without a dashboard—you wouldn't know how fast you're going, how much fuel you have left, or when the engine is overheating. In the same way, if you're not tracking the right metrics in your sales process, you're flying blind. To optimize your sales efforts, you need to know what's working, where things are stalling, and what needs adjustment.

With so much data available, the question becomes, which metrics matter? Here's a breakdown of the key metrics you should be tracking to ensure that each step of your sales process is running at peak performance.

Conversion rates

This metric tells you how many prospects success-fully move from one stage of your sales process to the next. Specifically, it would be best if you were tracking conversion rates from:

- **Contact to need.** How many leads move from the initial engagement to a meaningful discovery conversation?

- **Need to solution.** How many prospects move from identifying a need to hearing your solution?

- **Solution to negotiation.** How many prospects progress from hearing your solution to negotiating the terms?

- **Negotiation to close.** How many deals are successfully closed?

Why it matters

High conversion rates indicate your sales process is smooth and effective at moving prospects down the funnel. Low conversion rates suggest that some-thing's going wrong at specific stages—maybe your outreach isn't resonating, or your solution isn't posi-tioned clearly enough.

You can pinpoint where prospects drop off by track-ing these rates and making the necessary adjustments.

OPTIMIZATION TIP

Focus on improving the conversion rates at each stage.

If you're losing a lot of prospects early on, refine your lead generation and contact strategies. If the problem arises later, consider your qualifications or how you present your solution.

Average time spent in each stage

This metric tracks how long, on average, a prospect spends in each stage of the sales process—whether it's the time between initial contact and discovery, or the time it takes them to move from you presenting the solution to closing the deal.

Why it matters

The longer a deal sits in your pipeline, the more likely it will stall or fall apart. You can identify bottlenecks and inefficiencies by tracking the average time spent in each stage.

For instance, if prospects consistently get stuck in the negotiation phase, it might indicate a pricing issue or unclear terms. If prospects spend too much time evaluating your solution, try offering clearer, more compelling proposals that make it easier for them to decide.

OPTIMIZATION TIP

Set time benchmarks for each stage and work to streamline your process.

Shortening the time prospects spend in each stage can significantly impact the overall efficiency of your process.

Deal close rate

This is the percentage of deals that successfully close after reaching the final negotiation stage. It's the ultimate measure of success—how many deals you win.

Why it matters

A low close rate could signal several issues—perhaps your product or pricing isn't competitive, or your sales team isn't overcoming objections effectively. Tracking this metric helps you understand how well your team is closing deals and whether there are issues in the final stages of your sales process.

OPTIMIZATION TIP

Improve your close rate by focusing on objection handling and negotiation strategies.

Ensure your sales team is trained to address common objections and offer flexible, appealing terms that make it easy for prospects to say yes. Don't be afraid to analyze why specific deals are lost and learn from those failures to improve future negotiations.

Customer lifetime value (CLTV)

CLTV measures a customer's total value to your business throughout your relationship with them, from the first sale to any repeat business or upselling opportunities.

Why it matters

While closing deals is important, focusing only on the initial sale can be short-sighted. CLTV gives you a broader view of a customer's long-term value, helping you understand which customers are most profitable. This metric also allows you to align your sales and marketing efforts toward acquiring and retaining high-value clients.

OPTIMIZATION TIP

Optimize for long-term success, not just quick wins.

Ensure your sales process is designed to attract customers with high CLTV potential. For example, focus on industries or client segments more likely to repeat purchases or upsell. Use this metric to refine your targeting and qualification processes, ensuring you're not just closing deals but building lasting, profitable relationships.

Tracking the right metrics gives you visibility into what's working and what's not in your sales process. With this data, you can make informed decisions, test new strategies, and continually refine your approach to improve efficiency and close more deals.

Metrics don't just tell you what's happening—they give you the roadmap to sales success.

Iterating for continuous improvement

Optimization isn't just a checkbox on your to-do list in the fast-paced sales world—it's an ongoing journey.

Think of your sales process as a living organism, constantly adapting and evolving in response to new data, market conditions, and customer feedback. Like a finely tuned machine, every aspect of your sales strategy needs regular check-ups and adjustments to ensure peak performance. The key to sustained success lies in your ability to iterate based on the insights you gather from your metrics.

To remain competitive and responsive to your prospects' needs, you must embrace a culture of continuous improvement. It's not enough to implement changes once and forget about them; you must continually evaluate what works and doesn't and refine your approach accordingly.

Adjust and test

Iteration involves experimenting with new ideas, processes, and strategies to see how they impact your sales outcomes. It's about being proactive and willing to try different approaches to find what truly resonates with your audience.

Why it matters

The sales landscape is constantly changing. Customer preferences evolve, new competitors enter the market, and technology advances. Your sales team must be agile and willing to adapt to keep pace.

By regularly testing and adjusting your tactics, you can ensure your process remains effective and relevant.

Strategies for effective iteration

Test new outreach methods: Experiment with different channels for lead generation—whether it's social media, email marketing, cold calling, or networking events.

OPTIMIZATION TIP

Run A/B tests on your outreach messages to determine what resonates best with your audience. Try different subject lines, calls to action, or messaging styles to see which generates the highest response rates.

Modify your qualifying criteria: As you gather more data on what types of leads convert best, refine your criteria for qualifying prospects.

OPTIMIZATION TIP

Develop a scoring system that ranks leads based on factors like their industry, budget, pain points, and engagement level.

Regularly assess and update these criteria to align with your evolving understanding of your ideal customer profile.

Refine your offers: Your value proposition should evolve based on feedback and changing market conditions.

OPTIMIZATION TIP

Gather customer feedback after the sales process— whether through surveys, interviews, or follow-up calls—to understand how your offer was perceived.

Use this information to adjust your messaging, pricing, and bundling of services to better meet your prospects' needs.

Measure the impact of each change: Track the performance of any adjustments you make to determine their effectiveness.

OPTIMIZATION TIP

Set clear metrics to assess the success of your changes—such as improvements in conversion rates, reduced time spent in each stage, or higher customer satisfaction scores. Use this data to decide whether to fully implement or continue refining the changes.

The road to sales optimization is paved with continuous iteration. Adopting an experimentation mindset and being willing to adjust your strategies based on real-time data and insights can foster a culture of ongoing improvement. This commitment to iteration enhances your sales process and positions your team to thrive in an ever-evolving marketplace.

10
Ensuring A
Healthy Pipeline

Are you confident your company has a robust sales pipeline, or are you constantly worrying about potential gaps? Every executive dreams of steering a healthy, thriving, and stable company. What if the secret to achieving such a business lies not just in your product or service, but in the efficiency of your sales pipeline? How do you transform your pipeline into a machine that drives revenue consistently?

While having a competitive product or service is crucial, the backbone of sustainable growth lies in maintaining a fully functioning sales pipeline. What exactly does a healthy pipeline entail, and how can you ensure yours is thriving?

To answer these questions, let's delve into the essential elements you must master.

Understanding the sales pipeline

Imagine trying to navigate your way through a city without a map. You might know your destination, but without a clear route, you'd waste time, take wrong turns, and risk never arriving.

That's what it's like trying to grow a business without a well-maintained sales pipeline. This is the lifeblood of your revenue system—it's a visual representation of the stages your prospects pass through on their journey, from being leads to becoming paying customers. Your pipeline guides your sales team, allowing them to track each opportunity from its inception to the final close. Every process step is accounted for, and a healthy pipeline ensures no opportunity slips through the cracks.

Every sales pipeline comprises distinct stages. These can vary slightly depending on the business, but they typically include:

- **Lead generation:** Identifying and attracting potential customers.

- **Qualification:** Determining whether a lead is worth pursuing based on their needs, budget, and decision-making power.

- **Proposal:** Presenting your solution to the qualified lead, often with pricing and terms.

- **Closing:** Finalizing the deal and turning the lead into a customer.

As prospects progress from one stage to the next, monitoring their progress is essential. Are most leads getting stuck in the qualification stage? Are too few deals making it to the proposal phase?

The flow of prospects from one stage to another gives you critical insight into the health of your pipeline and areas for improvement. A well-structured sales pipeline provides clarity and predictability. It helps you understand where your revenue is coming from, forecast future sales, and identify any bottlenecks hindering your growth. By maintaining a close eye on your pipeline, you can proactively manage the health of your business and ensure long-term stability.

Components of a healthy pipeline

What factors make for a healthy pipeline?

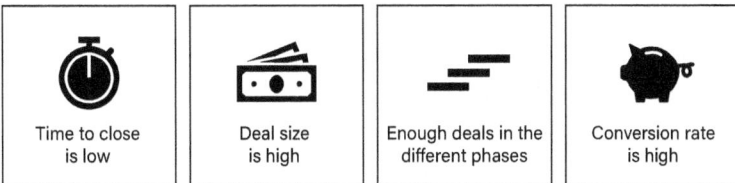

| Time to close is low | Deal size is high | Enough deals in the different phases | Conversion rate is high |

Four elements of a healthy pipeline

A low time to close

What if I told you that the time it takes to close a deal could be the difference between reaching your sales targets or watching them slip away?

Time to close refers to the time a lead takes to move through the sales pipeline from initial contact to final purchase. When that time is too long, it can create significant problems for your business—cash flow dries up, deals go cold, and growth grinds to a halt. A long sales cycle means your sales team is tied up chasing the same prospects for extended periods, leaving them little time to focus on generating new leads. Additionally, prospects can lose interest, priorities shift, or competitors swoop in with a better offer, causing you to lose the deal entirely.

Reducing your time to close is crucial to keeping the pipeline healthy and ensuring sustained growth.

Let's look at some strategies for reducing time to close.

Streamlining communication between sales and marketing

One of the most common reasons for a drawn-out sales cycle is a disconnect between sales and marketing. When marketing generates leads that aren't well qualified, the sales team wastes time chasing opportunities that aren't a good fit.

Improving communication between these departments ensures that only high-quality leads—those ready to buy—make it into the pipeline. Joint planning sessions, shared KPIs, and a feedback loop between sales and marketing can make a difference.

Implementing effective lead nurturing tactics

Prospects rarely make decisions immediately, especially in B2B sales, where buying cycles are longer and involve multiple decision makers. Lead nurturing is vital to keeping your prospects engaged and moving forward.

This involves providing the correct information at the right time to help them make an informed decision. Automated email sequences, personalized content, and timely follow-ups can nurture your leads and prevent them from stagnating in the pipeline.

Utilizing CRM tools for tracking and managing prospects

In the digital age, tracking prospects using spreadsheets or old-fashioned manual methods is no longer feasible. CRM tools offer real-time visibility into where each lead is in the sales process. They help you track communication, schedule follow-ups, and automate specific processes, all of which can reduce time to close. These tools can also provide data-driven insights into what's causing bottlenecks, allowing you to fix inefficiencies quickly.

By reducing your time to close, you free up valuable resources, create a smoother experience for your prospects, and increase the likelihood of converting leads into paying customers. Remember, a short and efficient sales cycle helps you hit your sales goals faster and gives you a competitive edge in a crowded market.

High deal size

What if you could double, triple, or even quadruple your revenue without chasing more leads? The secret lies in maximizing your deal size—getting more value from each deal you close. When you focus on larger deals, you better use your resources, close fewer but higher-value sales, and dramatically increase your bottom line.

How do you consistently win bigger deals? It all comes down to strategy.

Focusing on maximizing deal size isn't just about asking for more money—it's about delivering more value. Prospects will pay more when they believe you understand their unique challenges and can provide a solution that exceeds their expectations.

A bigger deal isn't just a financial win; it signals that your relationship with the client has evolved into a deeper trust and partnership.

Let's look at some strategies for increasing deal size.

Upselling and cross-selling techniques

One of the most straightforward ways to increase the value of a deal is through upselling and cross-selling. Upselling involves encouraging the customer to purchase a more advanced or premium version of the product they're considering, while cross-selling involves suggesting complementary products or services.

Think of this like adding toppings to a pizza order—when done right, it feels natural and improves the overall experience.

You must understand the customer's broader needs to upsell or cross-sell. During discussions, look for opportunities for your products or services to deliver extra value. For example, an upsell might be an advanced analytics package if a prospect purchases a software solution. At the same time, a cross-sell could offer implementation services or extended training for their team. The key is to frame these additional options as ways to solve more of their problems, not just as more significant price tags.

Building strong relationships to foster trust and larger commitments

High-value deals aren't won overnight. They come from building strong long-term relationships with your clients. Trust is the cornerstone of large commitments—when clients trust you, they're more willing to invest in extensive solutions because they believe you'll deliver.

Building trust takes time, consistent communication, and delivering on promises. Stay close to your clients and provide value even when you're not actively selling to them. Whether you're sharing industry insights, helping them navigate a challenge, or just checking in, these small touchpoints build credibility and deepen your relationship over time. As trust grows, so will the size of the deals they're willing to make with you.

Tailoring solutions to meet client-specific needs

No one wants a one-size-fits-all solution. The larger the deal, the more your client expects a tailored offering that meets their business challenges. By taking the time to understand their pain points, goals, and industry dynamics, you can craft a customized proposal that feels uniquely suited to them.

Tailoring your solution doesn't just involve tweaking product features—it could mean offering flexible pricing options, bundling services in a way that makes sense for the prospect's business, or providing additional support based on their requirements. When a prospect sees that you've built a solution just for them, they're more likely to sign a bigger deal because it feels like a perfect fit for their needs. Maximizing

deal size isn't about being pushy or overcharging—
it's about delivering maximum value.

Combining upselling, cross-selling, and tailored solutions with a trust-based relationship creates the conditions for more significant, more profitable deals.
Those big deals can be the game-changer that fuels
the growth of your sales pipeline.

Enough deals in different phases

Imagine your sales pipeline is like a relay race. Every
stage—lead generation, qualification, proposal, closing—represents a runner passing the baton. The
whole race is lost if one runner slows down or drops
the baton.

In the same way, a sales pipeline can only function
smoothly when there are enough deals in every phase,
moving forward consistently. If too many deals are
stuck at one stage or the top of your pipeline is running dry, the entire process grinds to a halt.

A balanced pipeline, with deals at various stages,
ensures you're never left scrambling to fill gaps. It creates a steady flow of opportunities moving from one
phase to the next, translating into predictable revenue
and stability for your business.

Let's look at some strategies for maintaining pipeline
balance.

Regularly reviewing the pipeline to identify bottlenecks

One of the first steps to maintaining balance in your pipeline is consistent proactive monitoring. You can't fix what you don't see, and bottlenecks in your sales process can go unnoticed until they become a significant issue.

Schedule regular pipeline reviews—weekly or bi-weekly—where you and your team assess where deals are getting stuck. Is there a particular stage where prospects tend to linger too long? Are deals frequently falling through at the negotiation stage?

By identifying these trouble spots early, you can implement strategies to unclog the flow and keep deals moving smoothly. For instance, if you notice a bottleneck in the qualification stage, your team might need more precise criteria for what constitutes a qualified lead. If deals are stalling at the negotiation phase, it may signal that pricing objections or contract terms need to be addressed earlier in the process.

Setting targets for lead generation to ensure a steady flow

Your pipeline's health begins at the top—with lead generation. A balanced pipeline requires a constant influx of fresh leads to ensure new opportunities are entering the process to replace deals as they close.

Without a steady flow, your pipeline will eventually run dry, and so will your sales.

To avoid this, set specific targets for lead generation at the start of every quarter or month. For example, you might establish a goal for the number of new leads your team needs to generate or a target for the number of outreach activities they should complete each week.

The idea is to ensure that lead generation is consistent and aligned with your sales goals so your pipeline never runs low. A consistent lead-generation strategy, whether through outreach, marketing campaigns, or referrals, helps create a sustainable flow of new opportunities. This reduces the pressure on any pipeline stage, giving your team the capacity to nurture and guide prospects without burnout or desperation to close.

Implementing a structured follow-up process to keep deals moving forward

Deals don't just move through the pipeline alone. They require consistent follow-up and nurturing. Too often, deals stall because sales teams lose momentum—they forget to follow up, miss key touchpoints, or fail to keep the prospect engaged. Implement a structured follow-up process with clear timelines and actions at each stage to prevent this. This could be as simple as setting up automated reminders in your CRM system to prompt timely outreach or using email sequences that nurture leads over time.

Your follow-up strategy should be focused on adding value at each step, not just pushing for a close. Send content that addresses the prospect's pain points, schedule check-ins to answer questions, and keep them engaged with personalized communication. A well-structured follow-up process ensures that no deal falls through the cracks. By staying top-of-mind and guiding prospects with clear next steps, you increase the chances of moving them forward through the pipeline and closer to the finish line.

Having a healthy pipeline isn't just about having enough leads at the top—it's about maintaining balance throughout. When you monitor your pipeline for bottlenecks, set clear targets for lead generation, and implement a structured follow-up system, you create the conditions for steady, predictable progress. That's the key to consistent sales success.

A high conversion rate

At the end of the day, the accurate measure of your sales pipeline's success is its conversion rate—the percentage of prospects that make it from initial contact to a closed deal. A high conversion rate signals that your sales process works efficiently, your messaging resonates, and your team executes effectively, but what if your conversion rates are lower than expected?

It could indicate that something is off, whether it's your approach to prospects, the quality of leads, or how well your sales team is trained to close. The good news is that conversion rates can always be improved by refining your strategy, focusing on the right opportunities, and equipping your team with the skills they need to seal the deal.

Let's look at some strategies for improving conversion rates.

Training sales teams on effective closing techniques

There's a certain finesse to closing a deal—a delicate balance of persuasion, confidence, and timing. While some people are natural closers, most salespeople need ongoing training to sharpen their skills.

High conversion rates depend on how well your team can guide prospects through the final stages of the buying journey and close the deal without hesitation. Consider conducting regular workshops or role-playing exercises focused on closing techniques. These sessions can help your team practice overcoming objections, negotiating terms, and building the trust needed to win commitments. Emphasize the importance of active listening during negotiations and teach strategies for addressing prospects' emotional and logical concerns before they make a final decision.

165

The goal is to arm your sales team with a toolbox of techniques they can rely on when the conversation gets tough. Whether they're handling last-minute objections, negotiating terms, or offering additional value, a well-trained sales force is critical to boosting conversion rates.

Personalizing communication to resonate with prospects

In today's competitive sales environment, generic one-size-fits-all pitches just won't cut it. Prospects want to feel understood, which means tailoring your communication to address their unique needs, challenges, and goals.

Personalization at every stage of the sales process is a powerful tool for improving conversion rates because it helps build a stronger connection between your team and the prospect. From the first contact to the final proposal, your team should craft personalized messages that speak directly to the prospect's situation. This might involve referencing a specific pain point they've mentioned, using industry-relevant language, or showcasing how your solution aligns exactly with their goals.

Personalized emails, phone calls, and presentations can dramatically increase engagement and trust, making prospects more likely to move forward with you rather than a competitor. By investing in personalization, you not only increase the chance of closing individual deals but also differentiate your company as one that truly understands its customers—leading to higher conversion rates across the board.

Analyzing lost deals to identify areas for improvement

Every lost deal is a learning opportunity. While it's easy to move on from them and focus on new prospects, analyzing why deals didn't close can provide invaluable insights that help you refine your sales process.

Conduct post-mortem analyses on deals that fell through, looking for patterns and common reasons for failure. Did the prospect cite pricing as an issue? Were there concerns about the fit or capabilities of your product? Did your sales team fail to address a critical objection?

Once you understand the root causes of lost deals, you can implement changes to address these gaps. For example, suppose you notice that prospects often hesitate due to price. In that case, you might need to revisit your pricing structure or highlight more value in your presentations. If prospects are getting cold feet due to a lack of perceived fit, your team could benefit from additional training on positioning your product or service more effectively.

Lost deals don't have to be dead-ends—they can become powerful tools for improving future conversion rates.

A high conversion rate is the ultimate indicator of a healthy, optimized sales pipeline. By training your team on closing techniques, personalizing communication to resonate with prospects, and learning from lost deals, you can continually improve your process and convert more opportunities into wins.

After all, success in sales isn't just about how many leads you generate—it's about how many deals you close.

Tracking key metrics for pipeline health

A healthy sales pipeline is built on data. Knowing if your pipeline is thriving or quietly withering away is impossible without tracking the right metrics. Leader in marketing research Gilbert A. Churchill (2010) highlights that consistent KPI tracking is essential for identifying areas of improvement and sustaining sales momentum.

Think of these metrics as the vital signs of your sales process. They tell you what's working, what needs attention, and where there's potential for improvement. The trick is knowing which metrics matter most and how to use them to make informed decisions.

Here are some key metrics for you to consider.

Time to close per stage

The amount of time a deal spends in each stage of your pipeline can reveal where things are flowing smoothly and where they're getting stuck. A short time to close indicates an efficient process. At the same time, long delays could signal issues with lead nurturing, qualification, or your sales approach.

For example, if prospects tend to stall in the need discovery phase of your sales process, it could mean your team is struggling to unearth the core problems they face. Similarly, if deals drag in the proposal stage of the pipeline, it might suggest that your offers aren't clear or compelling enough.

By monitoring how long deals linger in each phase, you can pinpoint bottlenecks and take action to move things along faster. The goal is to reduce time-to-close at each stage, keeping the pipeline flowing swiftly toward conversion without leaving deals to cool off.

Average deal size

How much revenue are you generating from each deal? Tracking average deal size is critical for understanding the overall value your pipeline is delivering. A healthy pipeline isn't just filled with deals—it's filled with high-quality deals that contribute meaningful revenue. If your average deal size is shrinking, it might be time to focus on upselling, cross-selling, or rethinking your pricing strategy. Conversely, suppose you see an upward trend in deal size. In that case, it's a good sign that your team is effectively selling larger solutions or successfully moving upmarket.

Average deal size is also a key indicator of your positioning in the market. Are you being seen as a premium solution worth investing in, or are you being pushed into the bargain bin?

This metric helps you answer those questions and adjust your approach accordingly.

Conversion rates from stage to stage

Conversion rates are the heartbeat of your pipeline. They show how effectively prospects move from one stage to the next—from initial contact to qualification or proposal to close. A strong conversion rate means your messaging and tactics are hitting the mark; a weak one signals trouble.

Tracking conversion rates at each stage lets you identify where prospects drop off. Are too many leads failing to qualify? Maybe your lead-generation efforts are attracting the wrong crowd. Are proposals going cold? It could mean your solution isn't aligning with the client's needs, or your pricing isn't competitive.

By measuring conversion rates at every step, you can fine-tune your approach and boost your chances of moving prospects to a successful close.

Overall pipeline value

Your pipeline's value is a snapshot of its potential to drive revenue. It represents the total value of all deals currently in the pipeline, which gives you an idea of the future income your company can expect if those deals close.

This metric is crucial for forecasting revenue and setting sales goals. Monitoring pipeline value helps you assess whether you're on track to hit your targets. If the pipeline value is too low, it's a signal that you need to ramp up lead-generation efforts or focus on closing more significant deals. If it's high but deals aren't closing, it could indicate that your pipeline is filled with unqualified leads or that your team is struggling to convert opportunities. Regularly reviewing pipeline value ensures you build steady revenue opportunities, not just a pile of wishful thinking.

Tracking these key metrics gives you a clear picture of your pipeline's health and the levers you can pull to optimize performance. Time to close, average deal size, conversion rates, and pipeline value are the cornerstones of an effective sales strategy. With this data, you can make smarter decisions, move deals through the pipeline more efficiently, and ensure that your company constantly drives toward growth.

Implementing continuous improvement

A healthy pipeline isn't something you set and forget. It's a living, breathing system that needs constant care and attention. Markets shift, customer expectations evolve, and competition gets tougher—if you're not adapting, you're falling behind.

To maintain a fully functioning pipeline, you must commit to continuous improvement, constantly refining your process to stay ahead.

Let's look at some strategies for continuous improvement.

Regularly reviewing pipeline performance and metrics

If you want to improve something, you must measure it. This means regularly diving into your pipeline metrics to evaluate progress. Are conversion rates steady, or are they dropping off? Is time-to-close improving, or are deals getting stuck in certain stages? Make it a routine to analyze these numbers, whether it's through weekly meetings or monthly reviews. By closely monitoring pipeline performance, you can quickly spot positive and negative trends and act accordingly. The faster you can identify issues, the quicker you can address them before they snowball into more significant problems.

Continuous monitoring helps you maintain an agile approach to sales, where real-time adjustments are made based on data rather than gut feeling.

Seeking feedback from the sales team on challenges faced

Your sales team is on the frontline daily, talking to prospects, handling objections, and closing deals. They're the ones who will notice the day-to-day challenges that might not show up in the data but could significantly impact pipeline health.

Make it a priority to regularly check in with your team and gather their feedback. Are they noticing any bottlenecks in the process? Are certain types of leads consistently harder to convert? What's working, and what's not?

Encouraging open communication fosters a culture of collaboration, where your sales reps feel empowered to suggest improvements. This feedback loop is essential for ensuring your pipeline evolves in a way that reflects real-world challenges.

Adapting strategies based on market changes and customer feedback

Markets change—sometimes faster than expected. What worked six months ago might not work today. Maybe new competitors have emerged, or customer preferences have shifted. Whatever the case, sticking to an outdated strategy in a rapidly evolving market can lead to a stagnant pipeline. To stay ahead, you need to be agile.

Regularly review your internal performance metrics and external factors like market trends and customer behavior. Are your prospects' pain points changing? Is your competition offering something new that's drawing interest? You can adapt your sales strategies to meet current demand by staying in tune with these shifts.

In addition, don't forget to gather feedback from customers. Whether it's gained through surveys, direct conversations, or post-sale reviews, customer feedback can give you valuable insights into how well your process meets their needs. Use this feedback to tweak your approach, offering solutions that are even more aligned with what your prospects are looking for.

A healthy pipeline isn't built overnight—it results from consistent effort, regular review, and a willingness to adapt. By focusing on continuous improvement, you ensure that your sales process is constantly evolving and capable of meeting new challenges and seizing new opportunities. Regular monitoring, team feedback, and a flexible approach to market shifts will keep your pipeline in peak condition, driving sustained growth for your business.

11

Achieving The Highest Win Rate Possible

What separates top sales performers from the rest? How do some organizations consistently close more deals than others, even when facing similar market conditions? It all comes down to one metric many obsess over: the win rate.

Here's the real question—are you winning as much as you should be? If not, what's stopping you?

Every sales team dreams of a high win rate. It's the ultimate measure of success, telling you how many deals you close relative to your number of opportunities, but improving your win rate isn't just about chasing more leads or applying more pressure to prospects. It's about selling smarter.

The key lies in solution selling, a robust approach beyond pitching products or services that offers tailored solutions to address a prospect's specific challenges. Sounds simple, right?

Achieving consistent success with a healthy pipeline comes down to getting five crucial elements right: power, pain, vision, value, and control.

$$W = P \times P \times V \times V \times C$$

| Win rate | Power | Pain | Vision | Value | Control |

Healthy pipeline

Master these, and your win rate will naturally soar.

Understanding a healthy pipeline

When most people think about sales, they picture the classic hustle: convincing prospects that your product is superior, beating competitors, and closing the deal. What if I told you that's not enough?

The real magic doesn't lie in just closing deals, but in closing the right deals. That's where having a healthy pipeline comes in.

A healthy pipeline flips the traditional sales mindset on its head. Instead of focusing on pushing your product or service, you shift the spotlight to the prospect and their specific needs. Author and consultant Neil Rackham (1988) introduced this approach, demonstrating its effectiveness in building trust and driving higher close rates.

In this model, you're not selling a product—you're offering a solution to a problem your prospect is struggling with. It's like being a doctor. The best doctors don't prescribe medicine until they've diagnosed the problem. Similarly, the best salespeople diagnose the prospect's pain before offering a remedy.

This approach transforms the sales process from a transaction into a consultative partnership. You're no longer just a vendor trying to make a sale—you're a trusted advisor helping the prospect solve their most pressing issues. Who wouldn't want to do business with someone genuinely invested in their success?

Why does this work?

Because it's human nature to make decisions based on trust and personal connection.

When prospects see that you understand their challenges and are genuinely interested in solving their problems, their defenses drop. They stop regarding you as a salesperson with an agenda and start seeing you as a partner who can help them achieve their goals.

Business sales experts Michael Bosworth and John Holland (2009) highlight in their book *CustomerCentric*

Selling the importance of focusing on the customer's needs and crafting a message that resonates with their challenges, rather than pushing a generic pitch. When you approach sales with this mindset, you're increasing your chances of closing a deal and building long-term relationships that can lead to repeat business and referrals. You're not just securing a win—you're creating a win-win.

The beauty of a healthy pipeline is that it ensures you work on deals where your solution truly fits. This means you're more likely to close deals that will succeed rather than pushing products onto prospects who aren't the right fit. It's about playing the long game, building trust, and positioning yourself as a partner that prospects can rely on.

In short, having a healthy pipeline is a strategy that benefits both sides. It allows you to align your offerings with the prospect's needs, driving more excellent value for them while increasing your chances of a win. In today's competitive landscape, that's a game-changer.

The five elements of a healthy pipeline

To master a healthy pipeline and significantly boost your win rate, you must nail down five critical elements: power, pain, vision, value, and control. Each plays a unique role in shaping the sales process, ensuring you're not just selling a product—you're navigating a complex decision-making ecosystem and presenting yourself as the best fit.

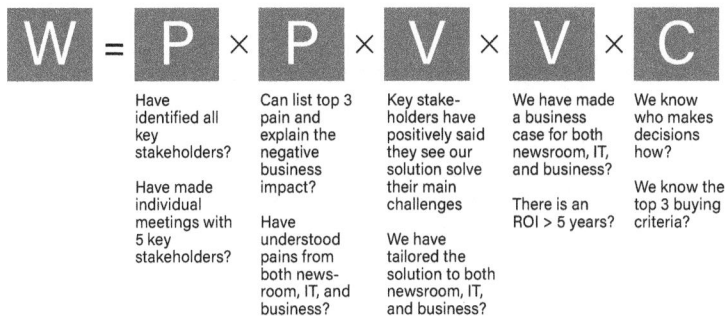

$$W = P \times P \times V \times V \times C$$

Have identified all key stakeholders?	Can list top 3 pain and explain the negative business impact?	Key stake-holders have positively said they see our solution solve their main challenges	We have made a business case for both newsroom, IT, and business?	We know who makes decisions how?
Have made individual meetings with 5 key stakeholders?	Have understood pains from both news-room, IT, and business?	We have tailored the solution to both newsroom, IT, and business?	There is an ROI > 5 years?	We know the top 3 buying criteria?

Mastering the healthy pipeline

Watch the video: Go to https://salesmarketingmastery.com/video/healthy-pipeline or scan the QR code for insights and inspiration.

Let's break these elements down, starting with power.

Power

Imagine this: you've spent weeks, maybe months working on a deal with someone who seems to love everything you offer. They nod in agreement during your presentations, share your enthusiasm for your solution, and even tell you it's exactly what their company needs. However, when it's time to sign on the dotted line, the deal stalls.

Why? Because the person you've been speaking with doesn't have the power to make the final decision.

In sales, **knowing who holds the power is essential**. It's not just about who's sitting in the room during your pitch; it's about understanding the entire web of decision makers and influencers that control the outcome of your deal. The worst mistake you can make is focusing on one person only to find out they don't have the authority to push the deal through.

Power isn't always concentrated in the hands of a single individual. In many cases, it's spread across multiple stakeholders, each with different levels of influence. You need to identify these players, understand their roles, and most importantly, learn how they make decisions.

Here's the tricky part: the key decision maker isn't always obvious. Sometimes, the person with the title or the corner office isn't the one who actually drives decisions. It could be someone in a different department or someone lower on the organizational chart who holds a lot of sway with the higher-ups.

Identifying these hidden influencers is crucial. That's why it helps to map out organizational stakeholders, as shown below.

Key questions to ask:

- Have I identified *all* key stakeholders, not just the most visible ones?
- Have I set up individual meetings with at least five key stakeholders to get a well-rounded view of the decision-making landscape?

Building relationships with multiple stakeholders is like laying down a safety net. If one connection falls through, you have others to catch the deal. Plus, by understanding the unique priorities of each stakeholder, you can tailor your approach and messaging to resonate with what matters most to them.

For example, the head of Information Technology (IT) might be most concerned about the technical compatibility of your solution. At the same time, the chief finance officer (CFO) might care more about cost savings and ROI. Speaking to both of their interests increases your chances of getting everyone on board.

Remember: power dynamics shift. The person who's driving the deal today might not be tomorrow. Stay flexible, keep track of changes in the decision-making structure, and adjust your strategy accordingly. By mapping out the power ecosystem and engaging with the right people at the correct times, you ensure you're not wasting time or losing deals to behind-the-scenes decision makers you've never met. Power is the engine behind every deal; your pipeline will stall if you're not connected.

Pain

At the core of every successful sale lies one undeniable truth: your prospect has a problem, and your solution exists to fix it. **Pain is the engine of change**. Without it, there's no urgency, no motivation, and no compelling reason for your prospect to move forward.

But identifying pain isn't always straightforward. Imagine walking into a prospect meeting and pitching your product's features—"Our software integrates seamlessly, saves time, and offers real-time insights." It sounds impressive, but without anchoring this to their specific pain points, your pitch risks falling flat. You're left with lukewarm interest at best.

Uncovering pain requires patience and precision. Start with broad, open-ended questions to encourage your prospect to share their challenges:

- "What's the biggest hurdle you're facing this quarter?"

- "What's holding you back from achieving your goals?"

Once they start sharing, it's time to go deeper. Use probing questions to explore the full extent of their challenges:

- "How does this issue impact your bottom line?"

- "What happens if this problem remains unsolved for another six months?"

Let's take an example. You're meeting with a manufacturing company that's struggling with downtime due to outdated equipment. On the surface, this seems like a straightforward problem. But as you dig deeper, you discover that:

- Downtime is leading to missed delivery deadlines, resulting in frustrated clients

- The production team is overworked, causing morale to drop

- The company's CEO fears losing market share to more agile competitors

Here's the critical step: quantify the pain. Perhaps downtime is costing them $500,000 annually, or customer churn is increasing by 10% each quarter. Numbers create urgency. They transform vague frustrations into a business case for action.

To look at another example: suppose your prospect says, "Our sales team isn't hitting their numbers." Don't stop there. Ask, "Why?" You may uncover that their CRM system is outdated, making it impossible to track leads effectively. Or perhaps their training program is misaligned with the skills needed to sell in today's market.

Lastly, remember that pain is rarely felt uniformly. Different stakeholders experience challenges from unique perspectives:

- For the CFO, pain might be increased operational costs.

- For the COO, it might be inefficiencies in the production line.

- For frontline managers, it might be team frustration or high turnover.

Your ability to connect these dots and present a cohesive story around the pain will set you apart.

Key questions to ask:

- Have I identified the most pressing pain points across departments?

- Have I quantified the pain in terms of cost, time, or missed opportunities?

- Am I tailoring my narrative to each stakeholder's unique perspective?

Vision

When you're closing deals, helping your prospect see the future is vital. Vision isn't just about telling them your product or service is good; it's about showing them how their world will transform once their challenges are resolved, specifically with your solution in place. It's the ability to paint a picture so vivid and compelling that the prospect can't help but imagine themselves there.

Here's the thing—**vision is personal**.

If your pitch is generic, the prospect will tune out. If your solution sounds like something they've heard from every other vendor, they won't buy in. You need to help them visualize a better and tailor-made future to win.

Think of it this way: you're not just selling a product—you're selling an outcome. Not just any outcome, but one where their specific pain points have been eradicated, and their business is thriving. A well-constructed vision shifts the conversation from "What do you sell?" to "What will your solution enable us to do that we can't do right now?"

How do you create this vision? It boils down to two key actions:

1. Get stakeholders to see it

2. Tailor the vision to the prospect's unique needs

1. Get stakeholders to see it

You can't assume your prospect automatically understands how your solution will solve their problems. You have to guide them there.

Have vital stakeholders expressed that your solution will solve their main challenges? This is a crucial question because if the decision makers don't see the solution as a fit, they won't champion it internally. Here's where it gets tricky: stakeholders aren't always on the same page. One person's vision of success may look completely different from another's, especially when they come from different departments. For example, the IT team may want a solution that improves system reliability. At the same time, the newsroom is more concerned with speed and ease of use. Your vision must unite these different perspectives under a unified solution.

2. Tailor the vision to the prospect's unique needs

Generic solutions don't sell. What sells is specificity—when the prospect feels you've built this solution just for them. This is where true value lies. You'll have their full attention when you can show each department how your solution addresses their immediate pain and helps them achieve their long-term goals.

Customizing your vision for each stakeholder isn't just a nice-to-have—it's a must-have if you want to win the deal. You're not pitching one solution to a company; you're pitching different solutions to different people under the same umbrella.

Key questions to ask:

- Have vital stakeholders expressed that our solution will solve their main challenges?

- Have we tailored our solution to the unique needs of different departments—newsroom, IT, and business?

When you create this kind of tailored vision, you build confidence. Your prospect sees your solution as *the* solution—the one that perfectly aligns with their business goals and challenges. That confidence leads to greater emotional investment, and emotional investment drives decision making.

When you've mapped out their pain and you're guiding them through your vision of a better future, you're really helping the decision makers take ownership of the solution before they've even signed the deal. That, my friend, is how you set the stage for a win.

Value

At the end of the day, value is what seals the deal. If your prospect can't see how your solution delivers tangible benefits—both in the short and long run—they won't pull the trigger.

Value is the language of business, and it's your job to speak it fluently. This isn't about rattling off features or superficial benefits; it's about proving that your solution will have a **direct and measurable impact** on your prospect's bottom line.

Imagine you're the prospect. You're weighing multiple options. You might love the idea of a new solution. Still, you won't sign anything unless you can clearly see how it will improve your operations and financial outlook.

This is where the ROI comes into play. When you're talking about value, you must paint a clear picture of how the value of your solution far outweighs the cost, and more importantly, how it solves their specific problems in ways that positively affect the prospect's business as a whole.

How do you prove that value? Focus on two things:

1. Build a business case for each department
2. Proving ROI

1. Build a business case for each department

No two company departments think alike, meaning no two departments value the same things. The newsroom cares about speed, accuracy, and functionality. IT wants security, reliability, and integration. Business is all about cost savings, revenue growth, and efficiency. Your job is to speak to all of them—to build a case that addresses the specific needs of each department while tying it all together into one cohesive, value-driven pitch.

Have you built a business case that addresses the needs of the newsroom, IT, and business departments? If you haven't, you're selling a one-size-fits-all solution that will not fly. Each department's decision maker must feel like the solution was designed with them in mind. You must show them the unique value they'll gain by choosing you over anyone else.

2. Proving ROI

Everyone's looking for an ROI—the bigger, the better. It's not enough to tell the prospect that your solution will improve their business; you must prove it in numbers. How much will they save? How much more efficient will they become? How will their revenue grow as a direct result of your solution?

It will help if you remember that your ROI must make sense. If you're promising wild returns quickly, your prospect might raise an eyebrow. Be realistic. You'll have their attention if you can confidently demonstrate that their investment will pay off over a reasonable timeline—usually five years or longer. They'll stop thinking about how much your solution costs and start thinking about how much it's worth.

Key questions to ask:

- Have we built a business case that addresses the needs of the newsroom, IT, and business departments?

- Does the prospect see an ROI that makes sense (e.g., over five years)?

When you can clearly define value and ROI, the decision-making process shifts. The prospect no longer has to debate whether they should buy—they'll be asking you when they can get started.

Control

Once you've uncovered and amplified the prospect's pain and created a common vision, the next challenge is maintaining control of the sales process. Without control, you risk losing momentum or being sidelined by delays, indecision, or internal politics within the prospect's organization.

Control is not about being forceful; it's about guiding the process in a way that feels natural and collaborative. Think of it as being a trusted navigator for your prospect on their journey to a solution.

Consider this scenario. You've had a great first meeting with a prospect, and they seem enthusiastic. But then weeks go by with no follow-up, no progress, and no decision. What happened? Likely, the process lacked clear direction or urgency.

Control starts with clarity. Every interaction should end with a defined next step, for example:

- "Let's schedule a follow-up call for next Tuesday to review your team's feedback."

- "I'll send over a summary of today's meeting. Can we set a date to discuss the proposal?"

Control also involves anticipating obstacles. What's likely to slow the deal down? For example:

- Are additional decision makers involved who haven't yet been brought into the conversation?

- Is there a budget approval process that needs navigating?

- Are internal priorities shifting, potentially sidelining your solution?

Here's an example of proactive control. You're working with a prospect whose budget cycle closes in three months. Rather than waiting passively, you might say: "To ensure we meet your timeline, let's map out the approval process together. Who else needs to be involved, and how can I help you bring them on board?"

Another example involves managing stakeholders. Suppose you're selling to a tech company, and the head of IT loves your solution, but the CFO remains skeptical about ROI. Losing control here means letting this internal conflict stall the deal. Taking control means offering to host a joint meeting: "It sounds like we need alignment on the financial impact. How about I set up a session to walk through the numbers with your CFO?"

Lastly, control requires confidence. Confidence to ask tough questions, like:

- "Is there anything that might prevent us from moving forward by [specific date]?"

- "What are the specific steps we need to take to finalize this decision?"

Without these questions, you're leaving the process to chance.

Key questions to ask:

- Am I setting clear next steps after every conversation?

- Have I identified potential roadblocks and addressed them proactively?

- Am I engaging all stakeholders and ensuring alignment on timelines?

The power of value lies in its ability to transform uncertainty into action. When you make it crystal clear that the prospect is not just buying a product but making an investment in their future success, you're no longer a vendor—you're their trusted partner in growth.

Bringing it all together

Now that we've explored the five essential elements of a healthy pipeline—power, pain, vision, value, and control—it's time to see how they work together to maximize your win rate. Each element is a crucial piece of the puzzle, but their real power lies in their synergy. When integrated correctly, they form a cohesive winning strategy that increases your chances of closing deals and positions you as a trusted partner rather than just another vendor.

Imagine you're trying to close a deal without understanding the prospect's decision-making structure (power)—you could be pitching to the wrong person, spinning your wheels with someone who can't green-light the purchase. Think about pursuing a deal without fully grasping the prospect's key pain points—you might be offering solutions to problems they don't even care about while their real issues remain unaddressed.

Similarly, if prospects don't have a clear vision of how your solution will transform their business or an undeniable sense of value, you'll struggle to win their confidence. Finally, without control, you risk losing momentum or getting blindsided by the decision criteria you never asked about.

Let's break it down:

- Power ensures you're in front of the right people. Without it, you're wasting time.

- Pain gives you the leverage to show why your solution matters. No pain, no urgency.

- Vision paints the picture of what success looks like with your help. Without it, prospects can't see why they need you.

- Value quantifies the benefit of your solution, demonstrating that it's worth the investment. Without value, you're just another expense.

- Control ensures you understand the prospect's process and criteria, allowing you to navigate the sale effectively. Without it, you risk getting stuck or losing deals to unforeseen roadblocks.

The beauty of a healthy pipeline lies in its flexibility and tailored approach. It isn't a one-size-fits-all method; it's about listening to the prospect, understanding their unique needs, and positioning your product or service as the customized answer.

When you consistently get all five elements right, you're not just improving your win rate, but fostering long-term relationships and creating loyal customers who will repeatedly return to you. Winning deals isn't just about having a great product, but mastering the process.

By implementing the solution-selling framework, you're turning a chaotic and often unpredictable process into one you can control and optimize. You're no longer hoping for wins—you're engineering them.

The next time you find yourself chasing a deal, stop and ask: "Does the stakeholder I'm talking to have the power? Have I fully grasped their pain? Am I showing them a clear vision? Have I demonstrated the value of my solution? Do I have control over the decision-making process?"

If you can check all those boxes, you'll boost your win rate and become the go-to partner your customers can't do without.

PART THREE

CULTURE: THE KEY TO DELIVERING AN AWESOME CUSTOMER EXPERIENCE

It's one thing to sell a product or service. It's another to deliver an exceptional experience that keeps customers coming back. In the B2B world, where long-term relationships often determine success, an awesome CX is critical, so how do you ensure that your team isn't just selling, but creating memorable experiences?

Let's take McDonald's as an example. Does McDonald's serve the best burgers? Hardly. After all, the staff just chuck a piece of meat between two pieces of bread and sell it to you. What McDonald's has mastered is delivering a consistent and enjoyable CX. People go to McDonald's not just because of the food, but because they know exactly what to expect: fast service, cleanliness, convenience, and a standardized experience across the globe. That keeps the lines moving and customers returning, regardless of the competition. It's not about the best product, but creating the best experience.

In B2B sales, a customer's experience with your team can decide whether they choose to work with you again, recommend you to others, and remain loyal for the long haul. In other words, it's not just what you sell that matters, but how you sell it.

This is why culture is so crucial—it influences what your team prioritizes, how they engage with customers, and ultimately, the quality of the experience they deliver. Psychologist Edgar Schein (2017) emphasizes that strong organizational culture aligns employee behavior with company values, creating a consistent and positive experience for customers.

How do you cultivate the right culture within your team to ensure they deliver an outstanding CX throughout the sales process? It comes down to influencing three key areas: how your team thinks, feels, and acts toward the market. This section will dive deep into these crucial components to explore how shaping them can drive long-term growth and sustainability.

Let's get started.

12
Getting Your Team
To Think Right

What makes a high-performing team genuinely great? It's not just about following orders or hitting quotas—those are surface-level outcomes. To build a team that consistently excels, you've got to dive deeper. You've got to shape how they think.

Here's the challenge: most teams aren't lacking in skill or effort. What they often miss is a clear understanding of why they do what they do. Without this more profound insight, they might execute tasks efficiently, but they'll lack the strategic foresight to adapt, innovate, and take ownership of their roles. It's like asking someone to run a race without showing them the course.

The difference between a good sales team and a great one often comes down to mindset—aligning their thought process with the company's goals, strategy, and vision. When a team understands the why behind their actions, they're not just working—they're working with purpose. They see the bigger picture, and suddenly, everything they do becomes more intentional, focused, and impactful.

Think of it this way: you can give someone the best tools in the world, but if they don't know why or how to use them in the context of a larger strategy, those tools are wasted. In the same way, a team without the right mindset might have all the resources and skills, but they won't achieve the level of success they could if they fully grasped why they're doing things a certain way.

How do you get your team to think right? It starts with giving them the insights behind two critical elements we've already discussed: strategy, and structure and process. Once they understand why certain things should be done a certain way and how their work contributes to the company's mission, they'll begin to see the purpose behind their efforts.

This chapter is about shifting your team from simply doing tasks to thinking strategically. Once they're in that mindset, you've laid the foundation for something even more powerful—getting them to feel the company's mission and vision, which ultimately drives how they act in the market.

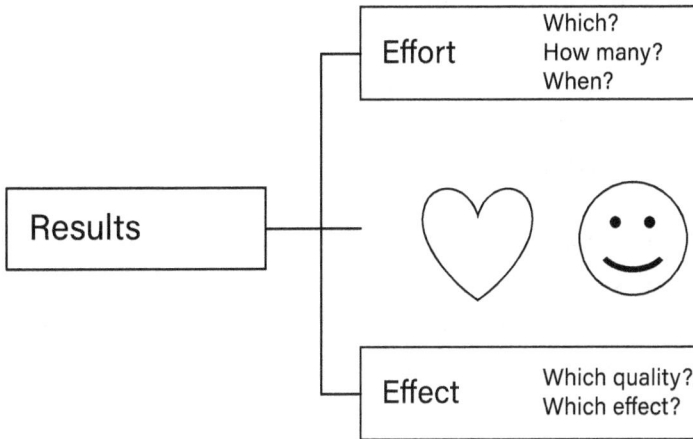

The tuning fork

Watch the video: Go to https://salesmarketingmastery.com/video/tuning-fork or scan the QR code for insights and inspiration.

Ready to get your team thinking right? Let's dive in.

The importance of getting your team to think right

Imagine a team that does everything right on the surface. They follow instructions, meet deadlines, and check off tasks, but if you peel back the layers, you might find they're merely going through the motions. Compare that to a team that executes well and understands the why behind every action. This is the difference between a team that completes tasks and a truly high-performing one.

When your team understands why specific actions are necessary—how their efforts connect to the broader company mission and vision—they stop acting like cogs in a machine and start thinking like owners. They understand the reasoning behind your strategy, and that clarity transforms how they approach their work. They become proactive, engaged, and invested in the outcome.

The way your team thinks directly affects their motivation, productivity, and overall effectiveness. A team that buys into the company's mission will go the extra mile because they see the bigger picture. They don't just do things because they're told to— they do them because they understand their purpose and value.

When you align your team's thinking with your company's strategy and structure, you empower them to take ownership of their roles. They become strategic thinkers, not just task-doers, and that's where actual performance and growth come from.

The link between strategy and mindset

Your company's strategy isn't just a document collecting dust in a binder—it's the roadmap to your success. Like any journey, everyone in your team must know where they're heading and why that destination matters. This is where the link between strategy and mindset becomes crucial.

To align your team's thinking with your company's mission, you must communicate the strategy in a clear, relevant, and actionable way. When your team understands how their roles and responsibilities contribute to the bigger picture, something shifts in how they work. Suddenly, their tasks stop feeling like isolated to-dos and become part of a more significant effort to move the company forward.

A team that sees the strategy as their guide will approach decisions with more intention and focus. They'll understand that each action they take has a ripple effect on the company's broader goals and that awareness will lead them to make smarter, more strategic decisions.

Key action points

Clarifying the strategy. This is the first step to ensuring your team knows the company's strategy exactly. Break it down into understandable terms, and show your team members how each task and action they perform directly connects to the company's broader goals. For instance, if your strategy is to expand market share, explain how their efforts in lead generation, client engagement, or customer service play into that vision.

Encouraging ownership. When employees understand their role in the company's success, they naturally take more initiative. They'll begin to act with purpose, knowing that their work matters. When people feel a sense of ownership, they stop waiting for direction and take charge of their impact. This shift in mindset can be a game-changer for overall team performance.

Helping your team connect their day-to-day work to the company's larger strategy transforms them from passive participants into active contributors to your success. It empowers them to think beyond their immediate tasks and focus on long-term growth.

Understanding structure and process for clear thinking

Structure and process are the unsung heroes of high-performing teams. Think of them as the foundation of a house—without a strong, clear framework, the whole thing could collapse.

When your team understands the structure and processes that guide their actions, they're empowered to work with greater clarity and efficiency. Without this understanding, confusion takes hold, focus drifts, and inefficiencies creep in, resulting in wasted time and missed opportunities.

A well-communicated structure allows your team to see where they fit into the broader system. At the same time, clear processes ensure everyone knows how things should be done. When they understand both properly, your team can proactively solve problems and anticipate challenges rather than reacting to them. They'll be able to confidently follow the established roadmap, reducing friction and bottlenecks.

Key action points

Educating the team on processes. It's not enough to have processes in place; your team needs to understand why they exist. Help them see that these processes are not arbitrary rules, but carefully crafted pathways to success. For example, if there's a specific way leads are qualified before they move through the pipeline, explain how this process ensures better alignment between the customer's needs and your product or service.

When your team understands the why, they're more likely to follow processes effectively.

Fostering efficiency. A clear understanding of the company's structure helps your team operate with fewer disruptions. It eliminates the guesswork of who covers what, where to turn for support, or how to handle specific situations. When your team knows the steps they need to follow, it removes the possibility of chaos. It creates a more streamlined, efficient workflow.

By aligning your team's thinking with the company's structure and processes, you set them up to operate at their best. Clear understanding creates a sense of order and control, allowing your team to focus on driving results rather than getting bogged down by confusion or inefficiency.

Communicating the company mission and vision

Purpose is one of the most powerful motivators in the workplace. When your team understands and fully embraces the company's mission and vision, their work becomes more than just a series of tasks—it becomes part of an extensive journey toward a meaningful goal. This deeper connection fuels motivation, engagement, and a drive to excel.

Your mission provides a clear sense of why the company exists and its purpose in the world. It's the compass that points everyone in the same direction. On the other hand, the vision paints a picture of where the company is heading, giving your team a glimpse of the future they're helping to build.

When these two elements are communicated effectively, they create a shared sense of purpose that ties the team's daily activities to long-term success.

Key action points

Mission alignment. Your team's daily work should reflect the company's mission. For instance, if the mission is to help businesses grow through innovative solutions, each team member should understand how their role contributes to achieving that goal.

Make sure that this connection is reinforced regularly—whether in team meetings, performance reviews, or one-on-one discussions. When employees see how their individual efforts support the bigger picture, they'll feel more empowered and committed to delivering results that align with the company's purpose.

Vision for the future. The company's vision inspires your team to think beyond the immediate day-to-day tasks. It gives them something to aim for—a future that feels tangible and worth working toward.

By showing your team how their contributions are directly building toward that vision, you can cultivate a mindset that's not just focused on short-term wins, but also on long-term success. This future-focused perspective helps your team think strategically, stay motivated, and invest in their roles for the long haul.

By clearly communicating the company's mission and vision, you create a sense of purpose that transcends individual tasks. Your team will be more aligned, engaged, and driven to contribute to a future they believe in.

Building buy-in for long-term thinking

Once your team understands the company's mission, vision, strategy, structure, and processes, cultivating emotional buy-in is the next essential step. This transition from understanding why things are done a particular way to caring about those reasons is critical for long-term success.

When employees emotionally invest in the company's direction, they become more engaged, proactive, and dedicated to achieving results that align with the overall objectives. A team that believes in the company's mission isn't just showing up to complete tasks—they're part of something bigger, which gives their work more meaning. This sense of purpose can significantly boost motivation, productivity, and retention, especially when the company faces inevitable challenges.

Emotional buy-in transforms a team from good workers to true partners in the company's success.

Key action points

Creating ownership. Building buy-in starts with helping your team members feel a sense of ownership over their roles within the bigger picture. This means encouraging them to view their responsibilities not just as assigned tasks, but as critical contributions to the company's long-term vision. When employees feel that their efforts directly impact the organization's success, they're more likely to go above and beyond, taking initiative and showing real commitment.

Ownership also fosters a deep sense of accountability. Team members who feel a personal stake in the company's success are more likely to be proactive problem solvers, willingly take on additional responsibilities, and consistently look for improvement.

Empowering decision making. When your team understands the underlying strategy and the processes that support it, they are empowered to make decisions that align with the company's goals. This autonomy enhances individual performance and strengthens the team's ability to adapt to challenges and seize opportunities.

Empowering decision making shows trust and respect for your team's judgment, boosting their confidence and investment in their work. It also allows them to act quickly and effectively without constant direction or oversight, contributing to smoother operations and better results.

Building buy-in and empowering your team to take ownership creates a workforce emotionally committed to the company's long-term success. This mindset shift drives sustainable growth, ensuring that your team is not just working hard, but working smart—with purpose, passion, and focus on the future.

Once your team members are thinking right—aligned with the company's mission, vision, strategy, structure, and processes—they're primed for the next step in building a high-performing sales culture: feeling right. This phase is where you move them from intellectual buy-in to emotional engagement. A team that understands the why behind their actions and feels connected to the mission is motivated, inspired, and capable of delivering exceptional CXs.

When people feel strongly about their work and its impact, their passion naturally translates into interacting with customers, handling challenges, and contributing to the company's long-term success. That passionate energy is contagious—it shines through to customers, influencing everything from the first point of contact to post-sale relationships.

By shaping the team's mindset, you've laid a strong foundation. Now it's time to cultivate a culture where they think clearly and feel empowered, valued, and driven to exceed expectations.

The next chapter will explore how to foster this emotional connection and why it's the key to driving outstanding CXs and long-term growth.

13
Getting Your Team
To Feel Right

Imagine a world where your sales team isn't just showing up to hit quotas, but each member is fired up, fully invested, and driven to go above and beyond. A world where they're not merely following a script, but bringing their best selves to every interaction because they want to—not because they have to. That's the energy you unleash when you tap into what makes your team tick.

Getting your team to feel right isn't about forcing enthusiasm or creating a temporary spike in motivation. It's about understanding what truly drives each individual—what gets them out of bed in the morning, what lights a fire under them—and showing them how their personal ambitions align perfectly with the company's goals. It's connecting their internal motivation, whether that's earning more money, advancing their career, or gaining recognition, to the work they do every day.

When people feel that their personal success is directly linked to their actions in the sales process, something powerful happens: they take ownership. They start to care about every interaction with a prospect, every follow-up email, every pitch—not just for the company's sake, but for their own. This is where passion meets performance.

When your team is emotionally invested, you've set the stage for higher performance and a culture that thrives on individual and collective success. The question is, how do you get there? How do you move from simply telling your team members what to do to making them feel excited about achieving their goals through their work?

In this chapter, we'll explore how you can tap into your team's emotional drivers, aligning their personal desires with your sales process to fuel individual and organizational growth. When your team feels right, they'll not only do more—they'll *want* to do more.

Understanding your team members' motivations

If you want your team to invest emotionally in their work, you must go beyond surface-level interactions.

It's not enough to hand out incentives or general pep talks—you must dig deeper and understand what makes each team member tick. What drives them? What do they hope to achieve, both personally and professionally?

At people's core, motivations can vary greatly. Some employees might be laser-focused on financial rewards—compensation goals, bonuses, or commission-based incentives. Others might seek recognition to feel valued and appreciated for their hard work. Some are motivated by the desire to develop new skills, climb the career ladder, or even make a broader impact on the world.

Understanding these drivers is the first step in getting your team to work hard with passion, intention, and excitement. Uncovering what matters most to each person opens the door to a more personalized leadership approach, and this personalization is critical. You can now show your employees in authentic terms how aligning with the company's goals can directly benefit them in achieving what they're after—whether that's hitting a sales target that results in a bigger paycheck, earning recognition for landing a major client, or developing skills that will propel them to the next level of their career.

Key action points

Uncovering motivations. Use one-on-one conversations, surveys, or even casual chats to learn what each team member cares about. Find out their career aspirations, financial goals, or personal values. Team-building exercises can also reveal insights into what drives them.

Personalizing your approach. Once you know what fuels your team members, you can tailor your leadership. Whether it's showing a commission-focused rep how following the sales process will lead to bigger paychecks or illustrating how gaining expertise will help a team member in their career advancement, personalization is the game-changer.

The clearer the link between their personal success and the company's goals, the more emotionally engaged your team members will become.

Linking motivation to success

It's one thing to understand what drives your team members; it's another to bridge the gap between those motivations and their day-to-day actions. This is where you turn personal desires into fuel for performance. To have their passion ignited, team members need to see a clear, undeniable link between their motivations and success in their roles.

Let's say one of your team members is motivated by financial gain. They aren't just showing up for the paycheck—they're focused on hitting high-commission targets, earning performance bonuses, and securing a lifestyle they dream about. It's your job to connect the dots between their desires and the actions they need to take.

This might mean breaking down the sales strategy and showing how executing each step of the process—making more calls, following up diligently, or building stronger client relationships—directly hits their targets. The clearer this connection becomes, the more naturally their motivation will transform into focused action.

For those driven by recognition, your approach might be different. You could demonstrate how consistently meeting sales goals or landing a big client can put them in the spotlight, opening up opportunities for public acknowledgment, promotions, or leadership roles.

The key is to make the path to team members' personal rewards evident and achievable. Once they can see how the dots connect, their effort feels worth it, and their commitment to the process strengthens.

Key action points

Connecting actions to rewards. Make it clear how individual performance directly impacts financial compensation, public recognition, or career advancement. Whatever their personal motivation, each team member must understand how following the proper steps leads to tangible results.

Motivating through clarity. Lay out the path to success in black and white. Show precisely how meeting or exceeding targets can help team members win personally—and leave no room for ambiguity. The more precise the path, the more motivated they'll be to walk it.

Creating emotional engagement in the sales process

To truly feel right, your team members need to be more than just physically present—they must be emotionally engaged. Emotional engagement goes beyond hitting targets and doing the minimum; it's about creating a deeper connection to their work and the team. This connection is the difference between a group of people going through the motions and a fully committed team that shows up ready to win every day. It's what transforms a job into a passion.

How do you create that level of emotional investment? You do it by fostering a sense of belonging and recognition. When your team members feel they're part of something bigger—critical cogs in the company's success—they take pride in their role and invest emotionally. It's no longer just about their paycheck or promotion; it's about being part of a team, contributing to a shared goal, and knowing that their work matters.

Recognition plays a huge role here. Everyone wants to feel seen, valued, and appreciated. By celebrating the small wins—landing a problematic client, reaching a monthly goal, or simply putting in extra effort—you show your team members that their contributions are noticed.

Recognition doesn't have to be grand; a simple shout-out during a team meeting, a personal email, or even a friendly pat on the back can go a long way. When people feel recognized, their sense of value creates loyalty and pride, and they're more emotionally invested as a result. This emotional investment is what fuels long-term performance.

When your team feels valued and connected, they will go the extra mile. They'll take ownership of their work, contribute ideas, and push through challenges—not because they have to, but because they want to.

That's when you know you've built a team that's not just successful, but also emotionally driven to excel.

Key action points

Fostering belonging. Build a strong team culture where every person feels like a critical part of the company's success. People want to be part of something meaningful, so create that sense of belonging.

Creating recognition opportunities. Regularly celebrate individual and team accomplishments, no matter how small. Acknowledge contributions publicly to show your team that their hard work makes a difference.

Driving excitement around results

The final step in getting your team to feel right is to ignite genuine excitement about the results they're working toward. When excitement builds, emotional engagement follows, which fuels consistent high performance.

It's not enough for your team members to understand the strategy or align their personal goals with the company's objectives—they need to feel energized and enthusiastic about the journey ahead. Excitement creates momentum. When your team is working toward their goals and excited about reaching them, it creates a self-sustaining cycle of motivation.

The key is ensuring their path to success feels real and attainable—something your team members can envision and rally behind. Whether that success is hitting revenue targets, earning a bonus, or reaching a personal milestone, you want to keep their focus on the big wins that await them.

One way to do this is by building enthusiasm through regular communication. Highlight progress in team meetings, use visual progress charts to track results, and celebrate wins, even small ones. Let your team feel the thrill of moving closer to their goals and the company's broader success. When the energy in the room is positive and contagious, it makes even the toughest challenges seem more achievable.

Additionally, you can use friendly competition to keep the excitement alive. Create an environment where team members push each other to excel, not in a cutthroat way, but through positive, constructive competition. Set up sales contests or leaderboards to add some excitement to the daily grind, ensuring that collaboration and team spirit remain intact even while competition is fierce. This keeps the workplace dynamic, fun, and full of energy—elements that are key to maintaining long-term emotional engagement.

By consistently generating excitement around results, you ensure your team stays connected to the mission, motivated to excel, and eager to celebrate their victories.

Key action points

Building enthusiasm. Keep the team energized by regularly communicating the excitement of hitting goals. Use tools like team meetings, visual progress charts, or incentives to celebrate progress and results.

Encouraging competition. Use friendly competition as a motivating factor, challenging your team to outperform themselves and their peers while maintaining a collaborative, team-focused atmosphere.

Now that your team members are emotionally engaged and deeply motivated, they're primed to move from understanding to action. When people feel genuinely invested—both emotionally and in terms of their personal and professional goals—they're ready to take on challenges with newfound energy and drive. This emotional alignment with the company's mission and its own ambitions becomes the foundation for action.

Let's talk about that next.

14

Getting Your Team To Act Right

Imagine this: you walk into a store and a salesperson immediately bombards you with questions, clearly eager to sell something—anything. Before you've even had a chance to explain what you need, they're off on a tangent about the features of their best-selling product.

Annoying, right?

Let's flip that scenario. What if instead, the salesperson took the time to understand why you walked in, what problem you're trying to solve, and what you actually care about? You would feel heard and be far more likely to buy from them because their recommendations would align perfectly with what you're looking for. That's the difference between salespeople who act right and those who don't.

In this chapter, we will explore how to get your team to act right by putting the customer first—understanding them, empathizing with their pain points, and guiding them toward a solution that genuinely benefits them.

How do you get your sales team to act right? It all boils down to shifting focus. For too long, traditional sales have been about hitting quotas, meeting internal targets, and pushing products. It's no wonder so many sales conversations feel transactional and hollow. Great salesmanship is a whole different story. It's about seeing the world through the customer's eyes. Instead of viewing a sale as a battle to win, you make the customer feel like you're on their side—helping *them* win.

This is where the *think, feel, act* model we've discussed comes full circle. In the previous two chapters, we explored getting your team members to think and feel right internally, but the real magic happens when they apply that same model outward toward the customer. They need to think like the customer, feel what the customer feels, and act in their best interest.

The sales team starts to do this by understanding the customer's world: what drives their organization's strategy, who the key decision makers are, and the business vision. Then, they must dive deeper and ask, "What motivates the customer? What are their fears, their desires? Is it the fear of falling behind competitors? Is it a drive to innovate faster?" By knowing these internal dynamics, your team can position your solution as something that directly addresses the customer's biggest challenges.

When your team can speak to those deeper motivations and show how your offer alleviates the customer's pain points, something powerful happens: your product becomes more than just another line item on their budget. It becomes the answer they've been looking for, the solution to help them succeed.

That's when getting the customer to sign on the dotted line becomes more than straightforward; it's almost inevitable.

This chapter's core is a simple yet profound shift in thinking: sales isn't about your product, it's about the customer.

The think, feel, act model applied to the customer

Imagine you're about to sell to a new client, but instead of jumping straight into your product's features, you take a step back.

> **Watch the video:** Go to https://salesmarketingmastery.com/video/green-track or scan the QR code for insights and inspiration.

You ask yourself: "What's this customer really trying to achieve? What are their core objectives as a business? Who's calling the shots on their end?" These questions form the foundation of a successful sales strategy because at the heart of every good sale is an understanding of who the customer is—not just what they need on paper, but what drives them.

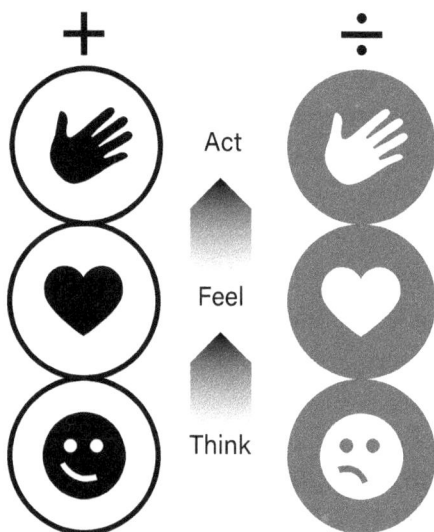

Green track: Think, feel, act

This is where the *think, feel, act* model comes into play. It starts with thinking like the customer. Your team must understand the customer's strategy, vision, and goals. Who are their key decision makers? What are their business priorities, and how do those priorities shape their actions?

It's not just about understanding what the customer is trying to accomplish, though. It would be better to go deeper to uncover what motivates them emotionally.

Every stakeholder within a company, from the marketing team to the CFO, is driven by different emotional triggers. For example, the marketing team might be motivated by FOMU. In contrast, the operations team may be focused on avoiding inefficiencies and keeping costs down. Once your team understands these emotional drivers, they can position your solution in a way that speaks directly to the underlying concerns.

Suppose the marketing team fears making serious mistakes. In that case, your team can highlight how your product or service puts those concerns to rest. If the operations team worries about inefficiencies, your team can emphasize how your solution will streamline processes and boost productivity.

When your pitch speaks to the customer's emotional needs and logical goals, the path to a sale becomes much smoother.

Key action points

Understanding the customer's strategy and mission. Identify the customer's core goals, business vision, and key stakeholders to tailor your pitch to resonate with their larger objectives.

Exploring emotional drivers. Go beyond surface-level needs to uncover the motivations and fears that drive decision makers, such as FOMU, growth ambitions, security concerns, or efficiency anxieties.

Empathy and perspective

Imagine your team stepping into the customer's shoes, looking around, and genuinely absorbing their environment. What do they see? What challenges do they face every day? By cultivating this kind of empathy, your sales team can transform their approach from simply pushing a product to genuinely understanding and addressing the needs of your clients.

Your team must identify their pain points and challenges to effectively connect with customers. What keeps them awake at night? Are they struggling with tight deadlines, budget constraints, or the fear of losing market share?

Understanding these worries isn't just about gathering intel—it's about developing a more profound connection that allows your team to respond to the customer's needs. As bestselling author Daniel Pink (2012) notes, understanding the customer's emotional drivers is key to creating a strong and lasting relationship. This perspective shift is crucial.

For instance, if a customer's marketing team is concerned about falling behind their competitors, your team should highlight how your product can help them gain a competitive edge. Suppose the operations team is dealing with inefficiencies that could lead to costly delays. In that case, your solution should be framed as the key to unlocking smoother processes.

By asking questions that reveal the customer's objectives and worries, your team can craft tailored solutions that resonate on both a logical and an emotional level. The goal is to position your offer not as just another product, but as a strategic tool that empowers customers to overcome their hurdles and achieve their ambitions.

Key action points

Customer-centric thinking. Train your team to think like the customer by asking insightful questions that uncover their concerns, ambitions, and the obstacles they face.

Positioning your offer as a solution. Frame your product or service as a direct answer to the customer's specific problems, illustrating how it can help them achieve their goals more quickly.

Tailoring the pitch to different stakeholders

In the intricate landscape of sales, it's essential to recognize that no two stakeholders within a company are alike. Each plays a unique role, with distinct priorities and concerns influencing their decision-making process.

For instance, the CFO is often laser-focused on cost efficiency and ROI. At the same time, the marketing team may be driven by innovation and the pursuit of growth. Understanding these nuances is critical for your sales team to act right and effectively engage with each individual.

To maximize their chances of success, your sales team must master the art of adaptation. This means tailoring their presentations to resonate with the specific priorities of each stakeholder.

Imagine a scenario where the CFO is presented with hard data showing cost savings and improved financial metrics. At the same time, the marketing team is excited to be introduced to cutting-edge features that could elevate their brand's visibility. Meanwhile, the operations team should hear about how your product will streamline workflows and enhance efficiency.

This tailored approach not only addresses the immediate concerns of each stakeholder, but also fosters a sense of inclusivity. When each person feels their unique needs and challenges are acknowledged, the sales process becomes a collaborative dialogue rather than a one-sided pitch.

By demonstrating that your solution can provide comprehensive benefits across various departments, your team can build a compelling case for its value.

Key action points

Customizing your approach. Train your team to adapt their presentations to meet the specific concerns of each decision maker, ensuring that they highlight relevant benefits tailored to their audience.

Ensuring comprehensive alignment. The more your team can demonstrate how your solution addresses the needs of every department, the more successful their pitch will be. This alignment increases the likelihood of closing the deal and strengthens relationships within the customer's organization.

AN EXAMPLE: Selling to a child through empathy

To illustrate the essence of great salesmanship, let's dive into a relatable everyday scenario that highlights the power of empathy and understanding motivations.

Picture a father trying to get his sixth-grade son to finish breakfast quickly so they can leave for school on time. The father feels the pressure of an important presentation at work and knows being late is not an option. He tries to explain the importance of timeliness. Still, the boy, oblivious to the father's concerns, is in no hurry to finish his meal.

As frustration builds, the father raises his voice, hoping to instill a sense of urgency in his son, but this only causes the child to become more defiant and upset, leading to a standoff where neither party is progressing, and the clock is ticking down to the last minute.

Then in steps the mother. She observes her son, noting the Superman T-shirt he proudly wears, which seems to mean a lot to him. With a keen understanding of her child's motivations, she asks him about the shirt, prompting the boy to share his excitement about impressing his friends at school with his favorite superhero.

Recognizing this key motivator, the mother reframes the situation. If the child finishes his breakfast quickly, they'll have time to get to school early, allowing him to showcase his shirt and bask in the admiration of his peers. She also reassures him that his father will be in a better mood once they leave on time, easing any lingering anxiety.

This simple shift in perspective is transformative. Suddenly, the child feels a sense of urgency—not from fear or frustration, but from a newfound excitement. He's motivated to finish eating to please his father and achieve something he genuinely cares about.

Before long, the boy finishes his breakfast, and he and his father leave the house right on schedule, with everyone satisfied and happy.

This scenario beautifully encapsulates the principles of effective salesmanship. By understanding what truly motivates the stakeholder—in this case, the child's desire for peer approval—the mother tailors her approach to resonate with his needs and emotions. This empathetic strategy leads to a desired outcome without conflict.

The same principle applies in sales: know your customer's motivations, speak to them, and frame your solutions to align with their goals. When you can connect on this level, closing the sale becomes natural and harmonious.

As service firm experts James L. Heskett, W. Earl Sasser, and Leonard A. Schlesinger (1997) emphasize, focusing on customer satisfaction leads to stronger relationships and higher sales performance.

Turning understanding into action

Once your team has effectively grasped the intricacies of the customer's strategy, feelings, and motivations, it's time to transition from understanding to action. This is the phase where the sales process becomes genuinely seamless.

By strategically positioning your offer as the best solution to the customer's problems and clearly demonstrating how it will help them achieve their goals, your sales team can craft an irresistible case for collaboration.

When they focus on how your solution can alleviate the customer's pain points and contribute to their objectives, the conversation shifts from selling to partnership. At this juncture, closing the deal transforms from a mere sales transaction into a joint effort toward shared success.

Key action points

Building toward the close. Equip your team to connect all the dots between their deep understanding of the customer's world and the tailored solutions they offer. This means they must articulate how each aspect of your proposal aligns with the customer's specific needs and objectives, creating a narrative that naturally leads to a close.

Positioning the offer as a partnership. Your team's approach should exude a sense of collaboration and support, making the customer feel like they are embarking on a journey together with your team rather than being pressured into a purchase. This partnership mentality not only makes the decision to buy easier, but also fosters long-term relationships built on trust and mutual benefit.

When your team effectively turns understanding into action, they drive sales and empower customers to see the value in what you offer. This shift toward a collaborative and empathetic sales approach can lead to more successful outcomes and enduring partnerships.

15
Sales Playbook

Now it's time for action. To help you take that action, I will provide you with a sales playbook. This is a guide that should help you create sales in the most efficient manner possible.

Download your copy: Go to https://salesmarketingmastery.com/files/sales-playbook or scan the QR code.

But before you get down to it, let me guide you on how to fill in its different sections.

> **Watch the video:** Go to https://salesmarketingmastery.com/video/playbook or scan the QR code for insights and inspiration.

Company description

Let's kick off with the basics. Ask these questions about your organization: "Who are we? What do we do?"

At its core, this section covers the foundation of who you are as a company. Start with your mission, vision, and promises to your customers. This isn't just fluff—it's the heartbeat of your business, guiding every decision you make and ensuring you're consistently delivering top-notch value to your customers.

In every internal meeting, you should come back to these guiding principles. Are you on track? Are you staying faithful to the promises you've made?

It's like using a GPS—your mission, vision, and customer promise help you stay the course, no matter where the road leads.

Example:

> "We're here to help athletes, both in football and handball, achieve their best—on and off the field. Our dream is a world where every one of our customers reaches their full potential. We're dedicated to giving them the strength and motivation to take charge of their lives and performance. Our promise: your ambition—our dedication."

Sales department, team, and roles

Sales isn't a one-person show. It's a full-blown team sport, with each player having a critical role.

Let's break it down. Who's talking to the customers? Who's prepping leads? Who's closing deals? How do all these roles connect?

Example:

- **Marketing** keeps a finger on the market's pulse and generates hot leads.

- **Pre-sales** reaches out to new leads and moves them forward.

- **Sales** engages with warm leads, closes the deals, and nurtures relationships.

- **Assembly** steps in post-close to ensure smooth setup and delivery.

- **After-sales** on boards customers and ensures they're always in the loop with the latest and greatest offers.

Knowing everyone's role is like running a smooth relay race—you win when the baton gets passed seamlessly. Once each role is understood and accepted by everyone on the team, you create efficient sales and unforgettable CXs, and when the customers win, everyone wins.

Ideal customer profile

Are all customers equally valuable? Nope! Not all customers are a great fit for your company; some can drain time and energy. The trick is knowing who your perfect customer is. The better you define your dream customer, the easier it is to attract and retain the ones that make your business thrive. Think of it like matchmaking—you want a perfect relationship where both sides feel the value.

Example:

> "Our ideal customers are machine shops in the metal industry. We work best with owner-managed companies that value close relationships and are always looking to optimize their operations. They're transparent

about their needs and appreciate a hands-on and forward-thinking partner. Most importantly—they understand that for both of us to win, we both need to make money."

Align your marketing, sales, and service efforts around customers that fit your ideal profile, and everything else gets smoother.

Map out your sales process

Your sales team should run like a well-oiled machine on precise processes. A defined sales process is your roadmap to success. It's not about perfecting everything—it's about consistently hitting your goals and knowing which behaviors drive results. Work with your team to outline the essential steps in your sales process, from the first lead to the final close.

Example:

- **Lead generation:** Marketing campaigns and social media buzz to bring in leads.

- **Contact:** Connect on LinkedIn and start the conversation.

- **First meeting:** Understand the prospect's needs and pitch the right solution.

- **Second meeting:** Dig deeper and fine-tune the offer.

- **Offer:** Send a proposal that speaks directly to the prospect's needs.

- **Close:** Seal the deal and celebrate the win!

When everyone knows what's expected, it's easier to replicate success—and spot where things might be going wrong.

Handling objections

Objections are part of the sales game. An objection is not a roadblock, but a chance to dive deeper into your customer's thinking.

Handling an objection, whether it's about price or product fit, like a pro can turn skeptics into believers. Instead of getting defensive, ask questions and understand the genuine concern. Then show the prospect the value you bring in a way that directly addresses their worry.

Example:

Objection: "You guys are way too expensive."

Response: "I hear you—pricing is definitely an important factor, but let's break it down. What's your biggest concern? If we look at the long term, how much would you save in service costs and reduced downtime with our product? Over seven years, you could save around $210,000—compared to an investment of $150,000, that's a significant gain. Plus, what other benefits do you see with our solution?"

Tools and technologies

In today's world, digitalization is non-negotiable. Everyone on the sales team must be on the same page about which tools to use and how to use them effectively. Tools can help streamline the process—but only if everyone knows how to use them well.

Instead of chasing after the latest shiny tool, focus on mastering the ones you already have. Provide training, share tips, and encourage your team to use tools to their full potential.

Example:

- **CRM:** Use XYZ CRM for all customer data entry [Link to system here].

- **Presentation tools:** For customer meetings, use the company-approved presentations.

- **Online meetings:** All virtual meetings are held via Teams, using the company's branded backgrounds [Link to background here].

KPIs and targets

Sales success is all about hitting the correct numbers, but you can't manage what you don't measure. What KPIs matter most to your team? Break them down into revenue, customer acquisition, and meeting targets.

Example:

- **Revenue:** Total revenue, revenue per customer, and earnings per customer.

- **Customer acquisition:** Number of outstanding offers in the pipeline, average offer value, and conversion rate.

- **Meeting targets:** Number of new customer contacts made each week.

Ensure everyone knows these KPIs and keeps them in mind. You can only stay on track and adjust by measuring the right things.

Daily, weekly, and monthly routines

Success doesn't just happen—it's built on consistent actions. To stay on top of everything, set up routines that become second nature. That way, you can focus on what matters without feeling overwhelmed. Create routines for checking in with customers, holding internal meetings, and reviewing your progress.

Example:

- **Daily:** Quick check-ins via Teams for any updates.

- **Weekly:** Sales team meetings to review KPIs and market challenges.

- **Monthly:** Personal follow-ups with all A and B customers.

Ensure these habits add value, rather than just filling up your schedule.

Tips and best practices

The best salespeople learn from each other. Share tips, tricks, and success stories across the team so everyone benefits. Whether it's a killer LinkedIn message or a winning objection-handling script, make sure it's easy to share and access.

Example:

"**Offer follow-up.** Before reviewing the offer with customers, send them a demo video and a product brochure. Then, during the follow-up call, ask them what stood out in the video. It's a great way to gauge interest and start a meaningful conversation."

Create a space—whether it's via Teams, Facebook, or another tool—where your team can swap ideas and keep the creativity flowing.

Additional resources

Your company is full of untapped resources—both human and technological. Ensure everyone knows what's available, whether it's access to a product expert or a lesser-known internal tool, and how to use it effectively. Having everything mapped out will ensure nothing slips through the cracks.

Example:

- **Marketing resources:** Product brochures, videos, and social media content.

- **Tech tools:** WeTransfer for file sharing and PDF converters for easy document handling.

- **Internal teams:** Reach out to research and design, quality control, and production for support on specialized topics.

A sales playbook is never a static document. It's a living, breathing tool designed to evolve as your business grows and the marketplace shifts. Think of it as a foundation you constantly reinforce with new insights, better processes, and innovative ideas.

The key to success lies in creating the playbook and actively using it, revisiting it, and refining it regularly. As your team learns more about your customers, competitors, and market conditions, make it a point to update your playbook. Include new best practices, address emerging challenges, and tweak your strategies to stay ahead of the curve. When used consistently and adjusted over time, the playbook becomes your most vital asset—a blueprint for excellence and a catalyst for long-term success. Keep pushing forward, keep learning, and keep building.

Conclusion

We started this journey with one simple truth: successful B2B sales isn't about luck—it's about having a clear, actionable strategy backed by a strong structure, process, and culture.

> **Watch the video:** Go to https://salesmarketingmastery.com/video/epilogue or scan the QR code for insights and inspiration.

Throughout this book, we've broken down the elements that make a winning sales and marketing approach in the B2B world. You now have the blueprint to transform your business by crafting a powerful strategy, aligning internal and external factors, embracing digitalization, and fostering a team culture that drives customer satisfaction. You've learned how to create a sales strategy that gets results, build a structure that supports efficient processes, and cultivate a culture that puts the CX at the heart of everything.

We've explored the power of understanding your customers deeply, keeping your pipeline healthy, and adapting to the ever-changing digital landscape. The chapters have laid out practical tips for everything from handling objections to utilizing the right tools and technologies. Now you have all the pieces in place, but remember, knowledge without action is just potential. It's time to take everything you've learned and put it into practice.

Start today by reflecting on your current approach, identifying where improvements can be made, and implementing the strategies we've discussed. Build a team that thrives on collaboration, continually seeks to understand the customer's needs, and consistently delivers exceptional value.

Success doesn't come from waiting for the perfect moment or figuring everything out in advance. It comes from taking that first step, refining, and staying committed to continuous improvement.

Take action now, lead with purpose, and let your business soar to new heights. Your company's future is in your hands, and with the right strategy, structure, and culture, there's no limit to what you can achieve.

Go out there and make it happen!

References

6Sense (2024) *The 2024 B2B Buyer Experience Report*, https://6sense.com/science-of-b2b/2024-buyer-experience-report, accessed January 23, 2025

Adamson, B. and Dixon, M. (2013) *The Challenger Sale: Taking control of the customer conversation* (Portfolio Penguin)

Bosworth, M. and Holland, J.R. (2009) *CustomerCentric Selling* (2nd ed.) (McGraw-Hill)

Churchill, G.A. et al (2010) *Sales Force Management* (11th ed.) (McGraw-Hill)

Cialdini, R.B. (2006) *Influence: The psychology of persuasion* (revised ed.) (Harper Business)

Covey, S.R. (2013) *The 7 Habits of Highly Effective People: Powerful lessons in personal change* (revised ed.) (Simon & Schuster)

Davenport, T.H. and Harris, J.G. (2017) *Competing on Analytics: The new science of winning* (Harvard Business Review Press)

Dixon, M. (2022) *The Jolt Effect: How high performers overcome customer indecision* (Portfolio)

Dixon, M. and McKenna, T. (2022) "Stop losing sales to customer indecision" (Harvard Business Review), https://hbr.org/2022/06/stop-losing-sales-to-customer-indecision, accessed November 29, 2024

Ellwood, M. (2017) "How sales reps spend their time" (Pace Productivity), www.paceproductivity.com/single-post/2017/02/09/how-sales-reps-spend-their-time, accessed January 23, 2025

Forrester Research (2021) *Forrester 2021 B2B Buying Study*, www.forrester.com/report/forresters-2021-b2b-buying-study-reveals-seismic-shifts-that-amplify-long-term-trends-in-buying-behavior/RES175653, accessed February 25, 2025

Gartner (no date) *B2B Buying: How top CSOs and CMOs optimize the journey*, www.gartner.com/en/sales/insights/b2b-buying-journey, accessed November 29, 2024

Gladwell, M. (2000) *The Tipping Point: How little things can make a big difference* (Little, Brown and Company)

Heskett, J.L., Sasser, W.E. and Schlesinger, L.A. (1997) *The Service Profit Chain: How leading companies link profit and growth to loyalty, satisfaction, and value* (Free Press)

Kotler, P. and Keller, K.L. (2019) *Marketing Management* (16th ed.) (Pearson Education)

McKinsey & Company (2021) *The B2B Decision-Maker Pulse Survey*

Miller, B. (2024) "7 marketing strategies to conquer decision paralysis" *(MarTech)*, https://martech.org/7-marketing-strategies-to-conquer-decision-paralysis, accessed November 29, 2024

Pink, D.H. (2012) *To Sell Is Human: The surprising truth about moving others* (Riverhead Books)

Rackham, N. (1988) *SPIN Selling* (McGraw-Hill Education)

Schein, E.H. (2017) *Organizational Culture and Leadership* (5th ed.) (Wiley)

Acknowledgments

Writing this book has been an incredible journey, shaped by years of experience, countless conversations, and invaluable lessons. As I reflect on my path, I am filled with gratitude for the people who have guided and inspired me along the way.

When I first graduated with a marketing degree from the Aarhus School of Business, I had no intention of pursuing a career in sales. However, life had other plans. I found myself in various sales roles, and one of the most formative experiences was selling software to accountants. Ironically, I was no expert in either software or accounting; my grades in both data and accounting were among the lowest. But I had one key strength: I knew how to show genuine interest in my customers. That simple principle became the foundation of my approach to sales.

A chance opportunity led me into the consulting world, thanks to my long-time friend of over thirty years, Jes Graugaard. Jes brought me into consulting, and together, we were part of the success story of Cultivator. It was during this time that my passion for sales and training salespeople and sales leaders truly began to flourish. Jes, without you, I would never have embarked on this journey into sales development. Thank you for believing in me and opening the door to this incredible field.

When Jes launched Intenz, I was fortunate to be part of the journey from the very beginning. At Intenz, I quickly took on the responsibility of developing commercial training programs. This was where I had the privilege of working closely with my incredible colleague and partner of twenty-five years, Rasmus Åradsson. Together, we created tools, frameworks, and strategies that have shaped countless sales teams. Rasmus, thank you for the many fantastic experiences at conferences and in the development room. Your partnership has been invaluable.

It was at Intenz that I first encountered the book *The Challenger Sale* by Matthew Dixon. This masterpiece ignited a fire in me and profoundly shaped my approach to sales. I have since had the privilege

ACKNOWLEDGMENTS

of meeting Matt, sharing the stage with him, and enjoying inspiring conversations over coffee and dinner. Matt, your work has been a monumental inspiration in my journey to master the art of selling. Thank you.

Later, I had the fortune of connecting with Karina Burgdorff. Her research into sales opened my eyes to the idea that "sales is not just sales." Sales methods and philosophies must align with a company's goals and the customer's experience. Karina, your insights and the inspiring network of researchers you introduced me to brought fresh theoretical perspectives to a practical field. Thank you, Karina, and thanks to your incredible network.

Over the past four years, I've enjoyed an amazing collaboration with Hans Løjborg. Hans is twenty-five years younger than me and a true inspiration for how sales and marketing can and should be done in today's world. Hans, thank you for keeping me young and challenging me to stay at the forefront of modern sales practices.

A heartfelt thank you goes to my wife, Helle, who has had to endure countless hours without me while I worked on this book. She has also patiently listened to many long conversations about B2B sales—perhaps not always the most riveting topic. Helle, your support means everything to me.

Lastly, I extend my deepest gratitude to all my amazing clients. Without you, I wouldn't have had the chance to test ideas, inspire outstanding results, and receive constructive feedback and challenges. You have been an integral part of this journey.

The Author

Mads Winther is a provocateur in sales and marketing with over twenty-five years' experience of turning potential into performance. From startups to corporate giants, he has worked across industries to inspire disciplined, value-driven sales strategies that benefit everyone involved. As an associate professor in strategy implementation and a founder of multiple companies, Mads has seen what works—and what doesn't.

He believes that sales isn't just about grit; it's about using your brain to craft smart plans. Because if you're not thinking ahead, you're already behind.

🌐 www.b2bclub.biz

🌐 www.intenz.com

▫ www.linkedin.com/in/mads-winther-19b8811

▫ www.facebook.com/mads.winther.566

www.ingramcontent.com/pod-product-compliance
Lightning Source LLC
Chambersburg PA
CBHW070349200326
41518CB00012B/2184